C000246785

The Map of Meaning
How to Sustain Our Humanity in the World of Work

•We have been applying aspects of the Holistic Development Model here in classes in management and leadership at Toi Whakaari New Zealand Drama School over the last four years. Students have found this frame an invaluable tool for orienting themselves in the face of what they see as an insurmountable range of paradoxes presented by our modern world. They ask themselves: how can I effect change ethically and meaningfully when my needs and those of the world, my values and the direction of society seem so at odds? Working with this frame has brought integration and empowerment, clarity and personal commitment to these students. It's great to see it now in its published form.•

Christian Penny, Director, Toi Whakaari New Zealand Drama School

•I read this book and did all the exercises in it. The book contains an indispensable tool to keep us whole. It will save us from burnout; it will save us from cynicism. It's totally non-judgemental. It's like a key that unlocks all that is important to us as human beings. As a consultant working in developed and developing countries, this framework gives me a simple way to profoundly engage with people across cultures. I can see for the first time not only myself but the context in which I live my life.•

Kerry McGovern, Public Sector Asset, Governance and Financial Management Specialist, K McGovern & Associates, Australia

•By providing a well-tested, comprehensive framework and language, this book helps managers to engage in a genuine dialogue on how daily tasks can be a natural expression of what truly matters, beyond profits and growth. Grounded and deep, the authors show us how to integrate inspiration and purpose into the reality of business.•

Lenette Schuijt, leadership trainer and author of several books on management and inspiration

‘I read this book with great delight. It is an important book, as it helps people orientate their career and work–life balance in line with their values and beliefs. It is a rigorous book, thoroughly researched and evidence-based, tried out and tested in various organisational sectors, in different countries and with a range of professions. It is also a 'dangerous' book, as it confronts readers with their innermost sense of being and challenges them to an intimate conversation with their self.

The human resource professional who wishes to work with human beings, rather than with human resources, will find in this book a useful and easily accessible tool, with numerous illustrations, to help people on their career journeys inside and outside work. It is very well written and deserves a good reception. Highly recommended.’
Yochanan Altman, Senior Professor, Bordeaux School of Management; Research Professor, London Metropolitan University; Visiting Professor, Sorbonne Universities (Pantheon-Assas); Founding Editor, *Journal of Management, Spirituality & Religion*; European Editor, *People & Strategy*

‘I loved your book and am so glad to have been exposed to your model and all the ways it can be generative—what a gift! Lips-Wiersma and Morris bring the meaning we make of life to a whole new level of understanding in their book *The Map of Meaning*. They offer their holistic developmental model as an analytical and practical tool for engaging different pathways of meaning-making in our work and in our lives more generally. The book is overflowing with useful advice and examples of how to engage the model as a means for fostering individual and collective growth, learning and re-becoming whole.’
Jane E. Dutton, Robert L. Kahn University Professor of Business Administration and Psychology, University of Michigan

•I had the good fortune of using this Holistic Development Model early in its development, both for my own growth and then in one of my classes. In my MBA class on Organisational Behaviour I use the model and describe it to the students as a sort of 'personal balanced scorecard'. The students immediately see its relevance to integrating their personal and professional lives. I am delighted to have this beautifully written book available, and if you are interested in your own growth as a whole person and/or if you assist others in that quest, you need to use this book.•

Douglas T. (Tim) Hall, Morton H. and Charlotte Friedman Professor in Management and MBA Faculty Director, Boston University School of Management

•The search for meaning is as old as humankind. The Holistic Development Model proposed in this sober volume is about learning to successfully engage the external world and its challenges from the inside. This is a contemplative yet practical work which is as incisive as it is revelatory. It combines our search for deep purpose with the need to align goals, aspirations and values within the environment we live in. It will be received as a welcome addition to the rich and growing literature on self-development irrespective of cultural boundaries. It is warmly recommended.•

Ramnath Narayanswamy, Professor in Economics and Social Sciences, Indian Institute of Management, Bangalore

•*The Map of Meaning* provides a well-structured and -tested framework for a reader who has the will power and tenacity to participate in a challenging ongoing conversation with one's own self and with others about how to create a meaningful life-path. The search for meaning is inclusive of a spiritual search where inner and outer realities interact to co-create personal and organisational existential fulfilment and make spirituality discussable at work. The book provides practical ways to work with this perennial human quest.•

Peter Pruzan, Professor Emeritus, Dr Polit. and PhD, Department of Management, Politics & Philosophy, Copenhagen Business School, Denmark; author of *Rational, Ethical & Spiritual Perspectives on Leadership* and co-author of *Leading with Wisdom: Spiritual-based Leadership in Business*

The Map
of Meaning

A guide to sustaining our humanity
in the world of work

Marjolein Lips-Wiersma and **Lani Morris**

Greenleaf
PUBLISHING

© 2011 Marjolein Lips-Wiersma and Lani Morris

Published by Greenleaf Publishing Limited
Aizlewood's Mill
Nursery Street
Sheffield S3 8GG
UK
www.greenleaf-publishing.com

Printed and bound by CPI Group (UK) Ltd, Croydon, CR0 4YY

Cover by LaliAbril.com

British Library Cataloguing in Publication Data:
     A catalogue record for this book is available from the British Library.

          ISBN-13: 9781906093655 (paperback)
          ISBN-13: 9781906093662 (hardback)
          ISBN-13: 9781907643439 (PDF eBook)

Dedication and acknowledgements

The search for meaningful work and a meaningful life is so pervasive that as we thought about both the dedication for this book and those we wished to acknowledge, we found that virtually every interaction had taught us something about what it is that makes work and life meaningful and meaningless.

To all those who nurtured our enquiry into meaning, our friends over our lifetimes, our colleagues, the people who participated in every aspect of our research, those pioneering contributors who courageously tried the work out on themselves and others, to the authors who have inspired and enriched us, our families who have supported us in so many ways, the students who so easily grasped the essence of meaning, the people who attended workshops and courses and argued with us, and all the ordinary people in the world to whom the question of meaning is so vital, this book is dedicated to you. We thank and acknowledge you with all our hearts.

Contents

1

Introduction, overview and welcome

> I had been given maps of life and knowledge on which there was hardly a trace of many of the things that I most cared about and that seemed to me to be of the greatest possible importance to the conduct of my life.

This was written by E.F. Schumacher (1978: 9), often referred to as one of the greatest thinkers of the 20th century, who was on a life-long quest to understand and communicate what makes life meaningful.[1] In this quotation Schumacher bemoans the fact that we so often lack the ability to pull the big picture of meaning and purpose into the choices we make in our day-to-day lives. Without such a map, Schumacher points out, human beings 'hesitate, doubt, change their minds, run hither and thither, uncertain not simply of how to get what they want, but above all of what they want' (Schumacher 1978: 14).

---

1 'To very few people', declared Barbara Ward in *The Times* on Schumacher's death in 1977, 'is it given to begin to change the direction of human thought. Dr Schumacher belongs to this intensely creative minority.'

In this book we introduce you to such a map, called the **Holistic Development Model**™, which provides a clear, simple and profound framework of the dimensions and process of living and working meaningfully. It helps you to define and stay in contact with what is most important to you as you grapple with the real problems of daily life. It helps you build your life on what matters most to you. It helps you work with the profound human questions that centre on: What *should* I do with my life? What should I do now? What guides me in living a meaningful life? and, How do I live and work as a responsible human being? And it does so from the big-picture level to the decisions and choices we are all faced with on a daily basis.

People who have used the Holistic Development Model compare it to the sort of map that Schumacher was seeking. To summarise what many of them say:

> The Holistic Development Model is like a type of a map, but actually the word 'map' is too static, because life is not static. It's dynamic. It's like a compass, or maybe more like a GPS (global positioning system) of the inner world, helping you to realign your purpose moment by moment. At the same time it doesn't tell you where you should go but, like a GPS, just offers insights from where you are about the endless little choices you have to make en route.

Like all reliable maps this one has been carefully tested. It is based on over 15 years' research into the insights and practice of ordinary people,[2] and although we borrow from the work of philosophers, psychologists and sociologists to provide evidence and context for our ideas, the main contribution of this book is that it describes how ordinary human beings wrestle with, and give answers to, the questions, What is meaningful work? and What is a meaningful life?

---

2 The initial research that laid the foundations of the shape and elements of the model has been well documented, initially in a PhD thesis (Lips-Wiersma 2000), and subsequently in peer-reviewed academic articles (Lips-Wiersma 2002; Lips-Wiersma and Mills 2002). Subsequent action research on the effects of the model has also been published in a peer-reviewed journal (Lips-Wiersma and Morris 2009), and an article quantitatively verifying the elements of the model and its universality is forthcoming in another academic journal (Lips-Wiersma and Wright forthcoming).

What we have found is that ordinary people, like you and me, have a good grasp on what makes work and life meaningful to them, but that they find it challenging to access this knowledge in the here and now and to speak about it and consistently act on it. As a result this innate knowledge about what makes our lives worthwhile is often not tapped into. The Holistic Development Model was developed by Marjolein Lips-Wiersma based on an in-depth collaborative process that enable research participants to make this knowledge visible to themselves. This was later followed by an extensive quantitative research project that found that people from a wide range of occupational and cultural backgrounds identified common meanings. The model captures and orders this common, innate human knowledge in a simple, profound and practical map that makes understanding and working with the key issues of meaning clear and accessible to everyone.

The purpose of this book is to help you access what you already know deep down but may struggle to bring to the surface and act on. It assumes that you, like your fellow human beings, are more likely to find your life and work meaningful when you pay attention to questions of meaningfulness and have a practical way to engage with them. It is for this reason that the book contributes to sustaining our humanity at work because working with the Holistic Development Model helps to keep the human search for meaning alive, especially in the face of the challenges that exist in organisational life.

The idea that there is a parallel between the meanings, decision-making dynamics and actions of individuals and organisations is central to the structure of this book. It is an old insight, as old as Plato (Goodpaster 2007), and yet is rich in significance for modern organisational life. This book therefore addresses meaning at both individual and organisational levels and in the dynamic between them. At an individual level, it will assist you to stay in charge of your ability to identify, create and sustain meaningful work and meaningful living. It helps you to discover specific areas of work and life that have meaning for you, and also those that lack meaning, and then to decide what to do. It supports you in voicing what is meaningful for you in ways that can be heard by a range of audiences including colleagues and superiors. For organisations, it enables people to have clarity of purpose with regard to what makes work and lives worthwhile while remaining flexible in response to changing circumstances. It offers ways to build and maintain workplaces that are meaningful to people and to make this an enduring change. It assists everyone to question organisational mind-sets and practices and find ways to let go of those that do not sustain our humanity. At the same time it encourages quick and purposeful action because working with the Holistic Development Model assists us individually and collectively to work and live as responsible human beings.

In the current economic context a simple map of meaning is essential precisely because organisational life has become so intensely directed towards a single economic goal that many practices have become dehumanising. It is vital that we have a simple and powerful way to reclaim the significance of meaning to human beings. There are numerous studies that show conclusively that meaningful work, or its absence, influences some important outcomes in organisational life such as work motivation, absenteeism, work behaviour, engagement, job satisfaction, empowerment, stress and performance (Rosso *et al.* 2010). Creating meaningful work therefore leads to many desired organisational outcomes, but implementing it does require the courage to question some fundamental ways of thinking about business and the integrity to engage with the issues sincerely.

However, this is not a naïve book. One of the strengths of the Holistic Development Model is that it takes tensions, paradoxes and imperfections as a given. They are part of being human. Tensions between Being and Doing; between the needs of Self and Others, between Inspiration and Reality are looked squarely in the face. They are all embedded in the tensions between material and the other human needs we have—such as the need for meaning. Being conscious of such tensions is an inevitable part of living meaningfully. Once treated as normal and shared, rather than denied, these tensions do not have to be overwhelming. We, and the organisations we work in, are not perfect: we and they never will be. We very often do not know what we are doing or why. At times we just struggle to get through the day. At the same time, as we find in ourselves and in many examples in this book, at any moment we need hope and idealism because we are capable of extraordinary transformative insight and action.

It is all part of being human.

Who should read this book?

This book is primarily written for those who are interested in creating more meaning and purpose in work and organisations, and who would like to better understand how to get others on board. It is for anyone who firmly believes that it must be possible to align our deeper life purposes with our daily actions. This is the purposeful CEO (chief executive officer), who knows what difference she wants to make but who, as with all CEOs, finds it hard to keep a steady gaze on what is most important when there are so many immediate issues to attend to. It is for the professional or blue-collar worker who knows what attracted him or her about the work in the first place, but who, as all workers do, gets lost in the systems of the organisation and can no longer connect with what is meaningful for him or her. The book is for those who work with and in organisations and who know that opportunities can be created and problems can be resolved by going deeper, not by doing more. It is for those searching for ways to re-energise their roles or change their careers. It is for those with high ideals who find it hard to find ways to speak about these ideas and put them into practice in their real lives and workplaces, and it is for anyone who finds that the maps they are currently using are no longer helpful.

In this book we talk about **meaningful work and life**. While the research was done on work and organisations, it is in the very nature of meaningfulness that it speaks to the whole person. What we learn and experience at work transfers to other roles and vice versa. The nature of meaning and the nature of the Holistic Development Model are both holistic and therefore will automatically draw into them, or be relevant to, many areas of life. So while in this book we focus largely on meaning at work, there are many examples of where and how people have used the Holistic Development Model in a wide variety of contexts.

In thinking about and working with the phenomena we describe in this book we contemplated several terms. We settled on 'meaningful' because it describes most precisely what the book is about. The meaning that we give to life is often based on our world-view, on what we believe about the purpose of life and afterlife. However, meaningfulness is not a belief. It describes the bridge that we create between what we believe and how we live our daily lives. Meaningful work is often related to the values we hold dear, but it is bigger than values in themselves. We can value a variety of things, such as having a lovely holiday or being successful or honest, but the word 'meaningful' asks the question behind this. It asks why these make your life more worthwhile. It is therefore more fundamental than values or intrinsic motivation (Chalofsky 2010). In searching for meaningful work you are likely to strive for some form of ideal, but meaningful work is not only an ideal; it addresses who we already are, and what we need for our work and life to be felt to be worthwhile in both our daily experience and in the sum of our lives. Finally, the words 'meaningful' and 'purpose' are often used interchangeably. We too do this from time to time. However, we do not refer to one ultimate purpose for our working life, precisely because we have found that there are many pathways that have purpose. For example, a purpose can be to fully express one's talents and a purpose can be to make a difference. In our model we include all of these pathways to meaningful work and life and also show the importance of understanding and addressing the right balance between them. Throughout the book we often simply refer to 'meaning' as a shortcut for 'meaningful' or for 'the meaning that we give to life'.

The first part of the book relates to your own search for meaning and how to share that with others. Meaningful living requires personal commitment, and it is important to stand strong in your own meaning. At the same time, it is also often true that if we 'put a meaningful person in a meaningless system' the system wins. Therefore in the second part of the book we cover meaningfulness in the wider context of the organisation. We link our findings to the premise that organisations benefit from people who are able to nurture and energise themselves, who are grounded in themselves, and who hold the institutions in which they work to account because they have high expectations of both themselves and the organisation. This part is also based on the premise that people and societies as a whole benefit from organisations where work is a natural extension of our search for meaning. This is therefore neither a self-help book, nor an organisational systems book. Its strength is that it draws together the aspirations of individuals, groups and organisations.

Meaningful work at your fingertips

To be human is to be in search of meaning. At some deep level we are defined as human beings by caring about what is meaningful to us. Yet the research that underpins this book shows that the answer will be different for each of us and will rise from each individual heart. At the same time, we are constantly in a process of finding and losing meaningfulness. We know when the quest for meaning is satisfied and we know when empty gestures, hollow words or manipulative techniques replace something that has had true significance for us. We don't really need to be told what is meaningful to us, so why this book?

At a personal level, although we yearn for meaning, we may not always pay attention to what is or has been most meaningful for us for us individually. While meaning is vital to us, at the same time it is easy to get distracted from what ultimately matters most to us. It is difficult to recognise or address the profound questions of meaning in our day-to-day existence given the speed at which our daily lives take place, and the conditions under which we work, all of which often detach us from what is meaningful. At the same time, questions of meaning often seem too 'big', abstract or irrelevant to the here and now. What is THE meaning of my life and of my work is, for many, just too overwhelming a question. So we end up not paying attention to these questions today and live as if we will, somehow, find the answers to them later on in our lives.

Our research has found that, at a personal level, working with the Holistic Development Model helps you to:

- Recognise and define what is truly important to you

- Find ways to talk about these to others, and listen to what is important to them

- See how the various things that are important to you relate to each other, so that you can make decisions that take all of these into account

- Begin to develop yourself as a whole person and so create an internal consistency, so that you feel deeply grounded in yourself

- Clarify the focus of your life and continue to clarify this as you and circumstances change over time

- Be increasingly able to be responsible for and in charge of your life and work

At a group level we may not feel comfortable talking about our deeper meanings or may simply not have the words to express them very well. Some of us may feel we are better off keeping what matters to us to ourselves and question if and when it is necessary and legitimate to take such information from the private into the public arena. After all, we have so many different world-views and these could lead to conflict, or someone could think we want to push our beliefs onto them. Yet if we cannot pay attention to and work with questions of meaning, meaning gets eroded from our work and life, and with it goes our humanity.

Our research and experience has found that, at a group level, working with the Holistic Development Model helps you to:

- Comfortably share what is meaningful to you and have meaningful conversations with others

- Understand the universal themes of what makes life worthwhile for each person while also being respectful of the differences in world-view

- Face challenges together in a way that allow you to work constructively

- Create respect and group cohesion at a deep level

- Identify energising ways of working together as you speak to what matters most

At the level of the organisation, even if people can define and stay connected with what is meaningful in their life, the complexity of the workplace seems to challenge so many of us to retain this connection. So often we get lost; so often we hear the haunting comments, 'But why are they making us do this? It's all so pointless! I can't understand it. As far as I am concerned it's a waste of time.' As academics and consultants working in the field of management, we have seen many great ideas and management fads sweep through organisations, offering some benefits, but ultimately contributing little of lasting value. Yet increasingly it is recognised that companies need to create deeper and more enduring mind-sets and practices.

We felt this book needed to be written precisely because to be human is not a fad. Being human is enduring and needs to be taken seriously. Human beings know what is meaningful and, for example, in the case of a mission statement, this knowledge needs to be accessed and articulated by the individual and be *expressed through* a mission statement rather than *prescribed by* a mission statement. It is not something that can be manipulated by the organisation, because what is meaningful is already deeply instilled in people. It is for this very reason that it is so vital that organisations understand meaningfulness (and meaninglessness) because members of the organisation evaluate every practice through it, even though they might not always voice this clearly to themselves or to others. We invite organisations to learn to work skilfully and wisely with this deeper aspect of our humanity.

Our need to have meaningful lives can form an enduring part of our experience of work; it can be taken into account in decision-making, teamwork, development practices and even in re-structuring, but it cannot be taken off the shelf and then returned as suits. There are many examples where meaning is used manipulatively in organisations. This doesn't work. For a person to be fully human and experience the fulfilment of satisfying work, he or she cannot be encouraged to put an individual sense of purpose (e.g. a desire to contribute to others) towards an organisational outcome (e.g. being asked to generously serve the client) and also be expected to disregard that same purpose if it is inconvenient for the company (e.g. being required to adhere to a rigid time allocation for customer interaction when real contribution would be achieved by taking just a few minutes more).

When the whole human being is brought into the workplace, the organisation will be examined by all employees through rigorous standards, and this requires substantial personal and organisational commitment. However, while attending to meaningful work does require time and commitment, it is also a sustainable way of engaging people. It does not take a complete overhaul of everything we have done before. It requires us to go deeper but it does not require us to do more; in fact, it often allows us to shed many useless and time-consuming practices. We may simply start to question a practice, such as performance reviews, client interactions or culture management practices, and ask: Which aspects make this a meaningful experience for all concerned? Which make it meaningless? and, How can we fix this together? Of course we can go further and ask, What is a meaningful purpose for the organisation? and in this way create a sustainable commitment to the organisational purpose. Or we can ask, What helps and what hinders us to stay collectively responsible for this purpose? This might lead us to go on to create sustainable leadership practices through a greater sharing of responsibility.

We have found that at an organisational level this book helps people to:

- Work together to create meaningful workplaces

- Re-energise workplaces and create a deeper level of engagement

- Arrive at vision and values statements that everyone buys into and for which everyone feels responsible

- Reclaim the significance of meaningfulness as a fundamental human need for people, organisations, communities and for society

- Expand and align the internal practices of meaningful work with the organisation's wider responsibility and sustainability goals

- And, as a result, work steadily, purposefully, collaboratively and sustainably

Meaningfulness has a profound effect because it restores dignity, responsibility and energy to each individual within the organisation. The content of this book provides a solid platform of understanding. With this understanding, practices can often be modified in subtle ways, once it is recognised which parts are humanising and which are dehumanising. This may not sound terribly exciting, but for those who have experienced the shifting sand that often results from endless, seemingly radical, quick-fix implementations of various non-integrated fads, we can promise that the question of what it is to be human at work leads to sustainable and systematic organising that is exciting because it supports our fullest engagement of our selves and this is needed as we take on the enormous responsibilities currently facing humanity.

So *how* does the Holistic Development Model help?

The Holistic Development Model does not come from, nor does it offer, a fixed dogma based on what human beings *should* do. Rather it is a framework that captures what human beings consistently consider *is* significant for meaningful work and meaningful life. It does not categorise people in any way; it does not try to fix them; and it does not impose world-views onto them. It returns each of us to our common humanity and from there supports our enquiry into what is truly important to us and how we can put that at the foundation of living and working meaningfully.

While it does not tell us what to do, it does provide a map based on universally acknowledged dimensions that together make for a meaningful life. This framework offers a basis for a range of exercises that can be used in a wide variety of ways. We describe a number of them in this book. You can use them on your own in individual reflection and enquiry, in one-on-one situations such as counselling or with friends and colleagues, or in small or large groups both within and outside the workplace. The Holistic Development Model, and the exercises we provide, can also be used to (re)design organisational practices and systems and we provide many examples of how to do this throughout the book.

Because the Holistic Development Model does not prescribe any specific belief, it is equally useful for people who have a specific faith, no faith or what has been described as a 'pick and mix' set of beliefs. For many of us who are not connected to any specific faith, it helps us to make sense of our beliefs and begin to examine them in relation to each other. For those with existing faiths it helps us to really live in accordance with our chosen faith. For all of us it helps us to pull our ideals, our beliefs and our spirituality into the daily physical reality of living and working and in this way keep in touch with our humanity in situations where this can be hard to do. To help you develop your skills in doing this we provide exercises in each chapter where you can try out the Holistic Development Model for yourself. We then report on the range of experiences others have had doing the same exercise and from these draw out consistent themes to help you think how you might go on to use the Holistic Development Model in your own life and work because for life and work to be meaningful we need to clearly understand the issues and questions that are at the heart of meaningfulness.

Throughout this book we also introduce a community of practitioners who have worked with the model in a wide range of contexts in a large number of countries (e.g. the United Kingdom, New Zealand, the Netherlands, Romania, Brazil and Saudi Arabia). They discuss how they have introduced the Holistic Development Model in different settings and generously share examples of their most effective exercises.

Their experience and our own over the past ten years gives us the confidence to now offer this model to a wider audience. It is tried and tested, backed by quantitative as well as qualitative data. It works both simply and profoundly. From it we have identified ten guiding principles central to creating and sustaining meaningful life and work and which form the foundation of the structure of this book:

1. **To create meaningful work we need a map that makes it easy to work with meaning.** The Holistic Development Model is clear and simple in its structure, easily grasped and easily used in a variety of forms, for example, on paper, on

the floor or in your head. It makes the dimensions and process of meaningfulness clear and easily understood (Chapter 2)

2. **To work with meaning we need to be able to first identify it for ourselves and next be able to speak about it confidently with others.** We show how the model helps you speak about what matters most to you and how to speak to each other about this in ways that make our differences and commonalities visible and lead to constructive action (Chapter 3)

3. **Meaning gets lost when we are out of balance for too long and opposing needs must be continually reassessed.** We show how the model helps us see and address fundamental tensions between the needs of Self and those of Others as well as between Being and Doing (Chapter 4)

4. **A meaningful life is whole and increasingly coherent.** We show how the Holistic Development Model helps you bring fragmented life and work experiences together into an integrated whole (Chapter 4)

5. **A meaningful life is a responsible life and we need to be able to stay in charge of what makes life meaningful for us.** We show how the Holistic Development Model helps us take responsibility for increasing meaningfulness for ourselves, and how we can co-create it with others (Chapter 5)

6. **For life and work to be meaningful we need to be both inspired and grounded in the real.** We show how the Holistic Development Model helps us stay in touch and reconnect with our sources of inspiration while staying fully connected to the reality of ourselves (including our imperfections) and our circumstances (such as the conditions in which we work and the economic conditions in which our work takes place) (Chapter 5)

7. **For life and work to be meaningful we need to be able to have conversations about what future, immediate or distant, local or global, we *do* want to create.** Attending to what is meaningful to us constructively engages us and

strengthens human dignity and power through a constructive engagement with future challenges (Chapter 5)

8. **Work can be far more meaningful if organisational conversations, practices and purposes support the human
   need for meaning.** If meaningful work is ignored, made
   invisible or in some way seen as inferior to an ideal of the
   organisation as an efficient machine, meaning is easily lost.
   Through a variety of case studies, we show how when meaning work becomes a foundational principle of organising it
   leads to responsible, realistic, whole-systems practices and
   structures in organisations (Chapters 6, 7 and 8)

9. **The responsibility revolution requires us to redefine
   the very nature of work and the purposes to which it
   is put.** In Chapter 9 we show how the dimensions of personal meaning are naturally in complete synergy with social
   and environmental responsibility. The model therefore aids
   in creating internal and external systems that are integrated
   and have integrity built into every aspect of organising.

10. **Meaningfulness is more easily achieved with others who
    are concerned with the same aim.** We look forward to a
    growing interactive community of workers, practitioners,
    leaders, trainers and consultants who work with the model.
    In Appendix 1 we outline how you can work with us and how
    we can work with you.

How should I use this book?

At the core of the book is the Holistic Development Model itself. In
Chapter 2 we briefly outline the research that underpins the model
and explain the key elements in detail so that you can fully understand it before we go on to work with it in specific situations later in
the book.

In each of the following chapters we introduce a range of exercises. We really encourage you to do at least some of them. The book

is not about the importance of living meaningfully; it is about how to do it. Learning how to do something can only be achieved by *actually doing it*. In the next chapters you will read stories of people who have worked with the model over a long time and in different situations. They continually stress how versatile the model is, how it helps them to analyse, speak to, plan around and respond to an enormous variety of issues and situations. It is this resourcefulness that we would like you to get from this book and have at your fingertips. But you will need to first work with and experience this model for yourself before you can convincingly share it with others.

In each of the chapters we also have sections in which we discuss what we and others have learned about this aspect of meaningfulness through working with the Holistic Development Model. And, since thinking about meaningfulness is as old as humanity, we put our experience and learning in the context of the writings of others.

Throughout, we provide references for those who want to read further. At the end of each chapter we summarise the key learning points.

From the feedback we have had so far, people prefer to read the book in different ways. Some choose to do the exercises first as they understand best through experiential learning. Others want to first obtain a practical or intellectual understanding and read the book before they do the exercises. Yet others are interested in particular segments of the book such as 'wholeness' or 'taking charge' and start reading here before finding out how these topics connect to all the others in the book. We invite you to read and work with the book in the way that best suits you. Most of all, we invite you to find out for yourself what difference working with the Holistic Development Model can make for you, because it only comes alive when you use it for yourself and begin to take control of creating more meaningful work and living a more meaningful and satisfying life.

To begin with, in the next chapter we will introduce you to the model that forms the heart of our work.

2
Background and guide to the map of meaning

In this chapter we introduce you to the Holistic Development Model. We do so in some detail so that you clearly understand the elements of the model before applying it in various contexts in the following chapters.

We begin by giving you a very brief background to the original research and how that resulted in the development of the model. Then we give a full description of the key elements that make up the framework of the Holistic Development Model, using many of the words of our research participants so you can see how it was built up from real life experience. You may recognise many of your own experiences in their words. To help you get to the heart of how you live each aspect of the model we include questions on each of its themes and sub-themes.

Background to the research at the foundation of the Holistic Development Model

In 2000, the first author, Marjolein Lips-Wiersma (2000), completed her PhD on the spiritual meaning of work. For the research component of this PhD she asked 15 people, of various occupational, ethnic and spiritual/religious backgrounds, to describe times when their spirituality and their work were aligned. On the basis of these stories, the researcher and participants together identified the elements of meaningful work: Developing the Inner Self, Unity with Others, Serving Others and Expressing Full Potential. These elements were then tested by the participants, who kept a diary to see whether their daily experiences of meaningfulness matched the themes. They did. However, one participant pointed out that meaningfulness did not only come from a combination of the themes but also from the right balance of them over time. This too was tested across the sample, and it was found that across all stories tensions and how these were addressed formed an important part of the process of meaningful working and living. On the basis of this feedback, Being and Doing and Self and Others were added and the first version of the model was completed.

After the original research had been presented in various management and academic contexts, people started to use the model in a variety of ways including as a blueprint for organising a conference and in courses on career management. At this point Marjolein and second author, Lani Morris, with their colleague, Patricia Greenhough, decided to offer workshops on the model. These took place in the United States, New Zealand, Australia, the United Kingdom and the Netherlands. During this time a second group of 230 participants took part in the testing of the model. With the aid of a research grant from the University of Canterbury (New Zealand) we systematically documented our findings on how the model made a difference in their lives. We subsequently published this research in the *Journal of Business Ethics* (Lips-Wiersma and Morris 2009).

The workshops offered an excellent opportunity to develop our practical and theoretical understanding of why this model was so

Figure 2.1 **The Holistic Development Model™**

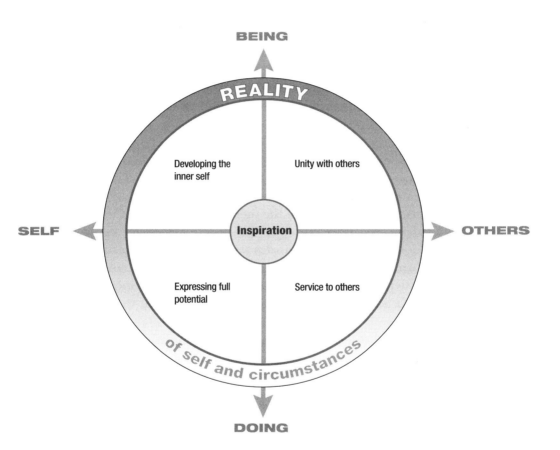

well received. We received invitations to run workshops and to use the model in a wide variety of situations: as the basis for courses, keynotes, lectures and academic articles; in one-to-one and organisational settings; and as a framework for personal reflection. All of these offered an excellent opportunity to develop our practical and theoretical understanding of why this model was so well received.

Added to this are the insights from a further 15 colleagues (academics, community workers, consultants, leaders, managers and coaches) who regularly use the model in their work. They have become a vital part of our enquiry as they actively participated in discussions on various versions of the initial framework and continue to test the model in practice. Their contribution forms a vital part of this book.

In 2010, again with the aid of a research grant from the University of Canterbury, we quantitatively tested the model on 500 participants from a wide variety of ages, occupations and cultures. The elements of the model, as well as their relationship to each other, were confirmed as capturing the content and process of meaningful work.

After 15 years of testing the model in this wide variety of ways, with a range of users and with an ever-widening group of participants in an ever-expanding range of countries we have reached a point where we are happy that the model in its present form is robust and useful. From this base we offer our understanding of the elements that make up meaningful work and meaningful living.

The elements of the model

There are three main aspects to the model.

The first is the **four pathways to meaningful work**; this shows us that human beings find meaning through the fulfilment of these four aspects of their lives. These are: **Developing the Inner Self**, **Unity with Others**, **Service to Others**, and **Expressing Full Potential**.

Second, these four pathways are held in **tension** by apparently opposing desires, the drive to meet the needs of the **Self** and the need to meet the needs of **Others**; and the need for **Being** (reflection) as well as the need for **Doing** (action).

Third, all these elements are played out in the overall context of **Inspiration** and the **Reality of our Self and our Circumstances**.

We will cover each aspect of the model in the next section.

The four pathways to meaningful work and meaningful living

In this section we give clear descriptions of the four main pathways that are the foundation of meaningful work and meaningful living. We describe each pathway as a whole and then describe the subthemes that make it up. For these we provide: a general description; a variety of words and stories used by the research participants; and some quotes to show that collectively human beings have always been engaged with this aspect of meaningfulness. We end with questions that we can ask ourselves and our organisations in order to understand the extent to which we are currently experiencing this aspect of meaning in our work.

Developing the Inner Self

This pathway, or quadrant of the model, refers to the meaningfulness that comes from active involvement with the person we are becoming as a result of being engaged in our life and work. Depending on one's world-view, Developing the Inner Self can be based on simply wanting to be a good person or the best we can be. Or, for some, it can mean getting the self out of the way, developing the self that God wants us to be, or becoming the higher self within us. Or it can be some combination of all these. At the heart of this pathway is the idea that an unexamined life is not worth living, and who we become as a result of being engaged in work, and in other parts of our lives, greatly matters to us as human beings.

People in workshops spoke about this pathway in the following ways:

To stay close to myself

Being a good person

To be ready to fulfil my role here

Being comfortable in my skin

Be the change you want to see in the world

I strive for love and harmony within my inner self

Courage/boldness of being who we are meant to be

The glory of God in a person is fully alive

Saying yes to the voice of God within me

We found that within the need to develop and become ourselves, there are three main sub-themes: **moral development**, **personal growth** and **being true to self**. Self-awareness is embedded in all three sub-themes.

Moral development

This aspect of Developing the Inner Self highlights the moral nature of our character and the ability of people to make a distinction between right and wrong.

People in workshops spoke about moral development in the following ways:

Honesty

Trustworthiness

Discerning the effects of my actions and interactions on others

Developing character

Being a good person

Having the courage to do what is right rather than convenient

Not compromising myself (too much)

An example of how people experienced this at work is: 'Currently we have many discussions about "what is the right thing to do here".'

Many sayings reinforce the universality and enduring relevance of this theme for human beings:

•• The sad truth is that most evil is done by people who never make up their minds to be either good or evil. •• (Hannah Arendt)

•• Great necessities call out great virtues. •• (Abigail Adams)

•• I know only that what is moral is what you feel good after and what is immoral is what you feel bad after. •• (Ernest Hemingway)

•• Two things awe me most, the starry sky above me and the moral law within me. •• (Immanuel Kant)

•• We do not act rightly because we have virtue or excellence, but we rather have those because we have acted rightly. •• (Aristotle)

•• Easy to do are things that are bad and not beneficial to oneself, but very, very difficult indeed to do is that which is beneficial and good. •• (Buddhism, Dhammapada: 163)

In order to think about how this aspect of meaning is playing out in our work/life, it can be useful to ask ourselves such questions as:

- When do I ask myself, What is the right thing to do? In what situations do I forget to ask this question?

- When did I last think about the right thing to do in a situation? When did I do the right thing? Why did I make this choice?

- How does what I think is 'right' relate to what others might think is 'right'—at work? in other areas of my life?

- What in my work encourages or discourages me to do the right thing?

- What are the conditions in organisations that support or damage moral development?

Personal growth

This covers both the idea of growth as deliberately 'cultivated', and the idea of allowing growth to come naturally into existence.

People in workshops spoke about personal growth in the following ways:

Expanding

Revealing insights and new ways

Developing my strengths and accepting my limitations

Awareness of skill and knowledge gaps and addressing these

Continuous learning

Being ready to fulfil my role to the best of my ability

Being responsible with my god-given talents

An example of how people experienced this at work is: 'With new responsibilities parts of myself emerged that I did not know I had. I was blossoming.'

Many sayings reinforce the universality and enduring relevance of this theme for human beings:

> ** You must learn day by day, year by year, to broaden your horizon. The more things you love, the more you are interested in, the more you enjoy, the more you are indignant about, the more you have left when anything happens. ** (Ethel Barrymore)

> ** To be what we are, and to become what we are capable of becoming, is the only end of life. ** (Robert Louis Stevenson)

> ** Of all the things that can have an effect on your future, I believe personal growth is the greatest. We can talk about sales growth, profit growth, asset growth, but all of this probably will not happen without personal growth. ** (Jim Rohn)

> ** Doest thou believe thyself to be a puny form, when the universe is folded within thee? ** (Baha'u'llah)

> ** The Master said, 'At fifteen I set my heart upon learning. At thirty, I had planted my feet upon firm ground. At forty, I no longer suffered from perplexities. At fifty, I knew what the biddings of heaven were. At sixty, I heard them with a docile ear. At seventy, I could follow the dictates of my own heart; for what I desired no longer overstepped the boundaries of right.' ** (Analects of Confucius 2: 4)

In order to think about how this aspect of meaning is playing out in our work and life, it can be useful to ask ourselves such questions as:

- If someone asked, can I come up with examples of how I have grown as a result of being engaged in this work?

- Am I becoming more or less ready to fulfil my role to the best of my ability?

- Am I still learning or am I standing still? If the latter, is that a conscious choice?

- What are the conditions in my organisation that stimulate, and stifle, personal growth?

Being true to self

This focuses on the aspects of not being false, being in accordance with the reality of oneself and being in perfect tune with one's self.

People in workshops spoke about being true to self in the following ways:

The freedom to be me

Being able to question

Privacy

Sticking to my own priorities

Uniqueness

Respect

Self-worth

Knowing my own mind

An example of how people experienced this at work is: 'I can be me in this organisation. I can dress in feminine clothes, be serious, be light, be me.'

Sayings that reinforce the universality and enduring relevance of this theme for human beings:

> °° Before his death Rabbi Zusya said 'In the coming world, they will not ask me "why were you not Moses?" They will ask me "Why were you not Zusya?" ' °° (Hasidic story)

" At bottom every man knows well enough that he is a unique being, only once on this earth; and by no extraordinary chance will such a marvellously picturesque piece of diversity in unity as he is, ever be put together a second time." (Friedrich Nietzsche)

" Just being yourself, being who you are, is a successful rebellion." (Author unknown)

" You might as well be yourself, everyone else is taken." (attributed to Oscar Wilde)

To check out this aspect of Developing the Inner Self you can ask:

- Am I becoming more or less myself as a result of being engaged in this work?

- When do I wear a mask? Why?

- When am I fully me? What are the consequences of being fully me, compared with being masked?

- What are the conditions in organisations that evoke our true self and which ones alienate us from our self?

Unity with Others

This pathway refers to the meaningfulness of living together with other human beings. Unity does not mean uniformity. It requires a balancing with other elements of the model to achieve unity but in diversity.

At the heart of this pathway is understanding that humanity is essentially one and that experiencing this is what enriches our humanity.

People in workshops put the following words to this pathway:

Being with my mates

It's all about teamwork

We can do more together than alone

Being part of a community

We are all one, the interconnectedness of it all

I am because you are

Living in and with and through each other, lives woven in love with each other

Synergy is the result of more than one person pooling energy

Iron sharpens iron—deep calls to deep. Maturity comes through interaction

See God in each other

In my experience our hearts connect when we talk about our deeper values, even though we might not agree.

Within the pathway of Unity with Others, we found three main sub-themes. These are: **working together**, **shared values** and **belonging**. Relatedness is embedded in all three sub-themes.

Working together

This sub-theme points to the sense that we can be more and achieve more with the support of others. Therefore it covers being in the company of others, to be combined in some way with others, so that one's power and resourcefulness are increased. And it includes the idea of mutual support.

People in workshops spoke about working together in the following ways:

Stimulation from others

Overcoming shared obstacles

Team

Fun

Mutually motivating

Energy

Feeling 'in kilter' with others brings validity to one's own work

Cooperation

An example of how people experienced this at work is: 'I probably would not have got into this line of work had my father not been involved in it. But Dad and I got on really well together, and I shared his enthusiasm for the business and the plans we had for expansion and it just flowed naturally from there.'

Sayings that reinforce the universality and enduring relevance of this theme for human beings:

> ❝ We must learn to live together as brothers or perish together as fools. ❞ (Martin Luther King Jr)

> ❝ As long as you keep a person down, some part of you has to be down there to hold him down, so it means you cannot soar as you otherwise might. ❞ (Marian Anderson)

> ❝ All is rooted in reciprocity. ❞ (Sri Yukteswar)

> ❝ Individually, we are one drop. Together, we are an ocean. ❞ (Ryunosuke Satoro)

> ❝ Every kingdom divided against itself is laid waste, and no city or house divided against itself will stand. ❞ (Matthew 12: 25)

And, again, we can check on how this aspect of meaning is in our lives by asking:

- Do I work with or against other people?

- Do I enjoy working together with my colleagues?

- Do I experience mutual support in my relationships at work?

- What makes it easier for people to work well with each other in my organisation? What gets in the way of people working well together?

Sharing values

This covers the concepts of articulating values, making values public and having values in common.

People in workshops spoke about sharing values in the following ways:

Making our assumptions visible

Shared conversations about values

Not having to justify things as there is a common understanding of our values

Sharing our knowing and our not knowing

Talking about why we do what we do before we actually go and do things

Making deeper conversation possible

An example of how people experienced this at work is: 'In my work I need to find some sort of bond with people, some common shared beliefs or value that you place on humanity in the broader sense of the word. And I get quite excited when I locate people like that at work because you don't come across them too often.'

A saying that reinforces the universality and enduring relevance of this theme in being human:

> First we talked about our purposes, then we agreed.
> (Mayan saying)

> Without commonly shared and widely entrenched moral values and obligations, neither the law, not democratic government, nor even the market economy will function properly. (Vaclav Havel)

> Grief can take care of itself, but to get the full value of joy you must have somebody to share it with. (Mark Twain)

> The power of a movement lies in the fact that it can indeed change the habits of people. This change is not the result of force but of dedication, of moral persuasion. (Stephen Biko)

> Set your expectations high; find men and women whose integrity and values you respect; get their agreement on a course of action; and give them your ultimate trust. (John Fellows Akers)

> The first step in the evolution of ethics is a sense of solidarity with other human beings. (Albert Schweitzer)

If you want to see how much you feel you share values with others, these questions might help:

- How often do we talk at work about why we do what we do?

- In my work, can I talk about what deeply matters to me? Can others?

- Do I sometimes choose to hide my values?

- Under what organisational conditions can we ask, Why are we doing this? What are our values and assumptions? What happens when we do?

Belonging

In this we see highlighted the idea of having the right to be a member of, being connected with, and being classed among, which points to the human need to be a part of a larger group with whom we feel deeply at home.

People in workshops spoke about belonging in the following ways:

Generosity

Warmth

Being part of

Being at home among

Acceptance

Not having to justify

Celebrating together

Feeling embraced

Community

An example of how people experienced this at work is: 'There are times when I look around at the people I work with and think how lucky I am to be part of this group, these people with such passion for the theatre, all these young people that are so dedicated, and the teachers who are so committed to the difference theatre can make. I pinch myself. It's like coming home.'

Two of the many quotes that reinforce the universality and enduring relevance of this theme are here from John O'Donohue:

> No soul/individual is sealed off or hermetically self-en-closed. Although each soul is individual and unique, by its very nature the soul hungers for relationship. Conse-quently, it is your soul that longs to belong—and it is your soul that makes all belonging possible. (2000: 17)

> The hunger to belong is not merely a desire to be attached to something. It is rather sensing that great transformation and discovery become possible when belonging is sheltered and true. (1998: 22)

Normally we know if we don't feel a sense of belonging, but if you want to think about it more directly you can ask yourself:

- Do I experience high-quality/deep connections with other people at work?

- Do I feel 'out of place' at work?

- Do I feel a sense of companionship at work?

- Under what conditions at work do people feel part of a com-munity? When do they feel alone?

Expressing Full Potential

This pathway refers to the meaningfulness of sounding our own note in the universe. It is different from Developing the Inner Self because it is active and outward directed, whereas the former is inward and reflective. At the heart of this pathway are the concepts that we are all unique, and that we are responsible for bringing our unique gifts and talents into the world.

The following quote from Marianne Williamson's book *A Return to Love,* and often erroneously attributed to Nelson Mandela, is as popular as it is because it so clearly captures both our longing and our anxiousness about expressing our full potential:

> Our deepest fear is not that we are inadequate. Our deep-est fear is that we are powerful beyond measure. It is our light, not our darkness, that most frightens us. We ask ourselves, who am I to be brilliant, gorgeous, talented and fabulous? Actually, who are you not to be? You are a child of God. Your playing small doesn't serve the world. There

is nothing enlightened about shrinking so that other people won't feel insecure around you. We are born to make manifest the glory of God that is within us. It is not just in some of us; it is in everyone. And as we let our own light shine, we unconsciously give other people permission to do the same. As we are liberated from our fears, our presence automatically liberates others. (Williamson 1992)

People in workshops spoke about this pathway in the following ways:

Doing my best work at all times

Being responsible for making the most use of my gifts and talents

The delight in knowing that I've done a good piece of work

Find out what you are good at and do more of it!

Freedom to express

Individuality in all its forms

Soulful writing, dancing, working

Every act is an act of will and therefore creative—conscious living

Sounding my note in the universe

Generally we found that Expressing Full Potential could be found in three main sub-themes. These are **creating**, **achieving** and **influencing**.

Creating

This covers the need to bring into existence, give rise to or originate.

People in workshops spoke about creating in the following ways:

Enjoyment of making things

Love of exploration and expression

Having an outlet to express me

Creative flow

Energy towards a vision

Adding my bits to the bigger picture

Beauty

An example of this in the workplace is: 'I pour my energy now into my oyster farm and that to me is social and economic development for the community. And the oyster farm is to me like my painting. I'm creating something in the area where oyster farming was always deemed unviable; we just decided we would make it work.'

Many sayings reinforce the universality and enduring relevance of this theme for human beings:

> ** A bird doesn't sing because it has an answer, it sings because it has a song. ** (Maya Angelou)

> ** Sometimes creativity just means the daily work of helping others to see a problem in a different way. ** (Joseph Badaracco)

> ** There is a vitality, a life force, an energy, a quickening, which is translated through you into action. And because there is only one you in all time, this expression is unique and if you block it, it will never exist through any other medium and the world will not have it. ** (Martha Graham in a letter to Agnes de Mille)

Though organisations and individuals know that creativity is valuable, it is useful sometimes to check on how much of it we are able to experience:

- Do I have times when I am so engaged with my work that I lose track of time?

- How much can I really apply my gifts and talents at work?

- Am I stimulated to be creative at work or discover new ways of doing things at work?

- Can I apply my new ideas or concepts at work?

- Do I get excited or enthusiastic about what we create?

- Under what conditions do people feel creative at my workplace?

- In what conditions do they choose not to contribute their unique gifts and talents?

Achieving

In this sub-theme we acknowledge the human need to accomplish, to carry things out to their conclusion.

People in workshops spoke about achieving in the following ways:

Benchmarking

Just do it

The meaning that comes from mastering something

Ambition

Recognition

Success

Completing

Competent

Effective

Improving standards

A work example of this is: 'There is an inherent meaning in mastering something. When something comes out of my hands that I know to be good, it is a great feeling.'

Many sayings reinforce the universality and enduring relevance of this theme for human beings:

"" My grandfather once told me that there were two kinds of people: those who do the work and those who take the credit. He told me to try to be in the first group; there was much less competition."" (Indira Gandhi)

"" When you practise excellence you are not trying to be better than anyone else. You are trying to be the best you can be."" (Linda Kavelin Popov)

"" Things were made like God not only in being but also in acting. Whatever causes God to assign to certain effects, God gives them the power to produce those effects."" (Thomas Aquinas)

"" Whoever I am and whatever I am doing, some kind excellence is within my reach."" (John W. Gardiner)

> ⁰⁰ Achievement seems to be connected with action. Successful men and women keep moving. They make mistakes, but they don't quit. ⁰⁰ (Conrad Hilton)

Questions you may want to ask yourself to get a sense of how much you feel you are achieving:

- Do I regularly experience a sense of achievement?

- Where and when is this not happening? What stops me?

- What do I long to achieve? What would be the first step to doing this?

- How often do individuals in my organisation have a sense of achievement?

- How often do they have a sense of failure? What causes these differing experiences?

Influencing

Influencing covers our need to affect destiny, or have in some way the power to bring something about.

People in workshops spoke about influencing in the following ways:

Getting others on board

Inspiring others

Reminding others of why we do what we do

Improving conditions for those less powerful

Offering direction

Drawing attention to important issues

Setting an example

Examples of how people experienced this at work are: 'In this role I can actively help shape the organisation', and in this story where someone was able to take a small action and solve a problem, 'We had a problem with the manager. But I went to see him and we got our trolleys back'.

A wonderful story that captures the creativity with which an individual can choose to influence is in Werner Herzog's autobiography.

> In 1974 we German filmmakers were still fragile, and when a friend told me Lotte (Eisner) had suffered a massive stroke and I should get on the next plane to Paris, I made the decision not to fly. It was not the right thing to do, and because I just could not accept that she might die, I walked from Munich to her apartment in Paris. I put on a shirt, grabbed a bundle of clothes, a map and a compass and set off in a straight line, sleeping under bridges, in farms and abandoned houses . . . I walked against her death, knowing that if I walked on foot she would be alive when I got there. And that is just what happened. Lotte lived until the age of ninety or thereabouts, and years after the walk, and she was nearly blind etc, she said to me, 'Werner there is still this spell cast over me that I am not allowed to die. I am tired of life. It would be a good time for me now.' Joking I said, 'OK Lotte, I hereby take the spell away.' Three weeks later she died. (Herzog and Cronin 2002: 281)

To test our sense of being able to influence we can ask:

- What can I influence?

- How much am I able to influence?

- What would I like to influence more? What could enable me to do so?

- What are the conditions at work under which every individual can have a say in the things that affect them?

Service to Others

Serving others is about the human need to make a contribution to the well-being of others, from helping an individual to making a difference in the wider world.

People in workshops spoke about this pathway in the following ways:

If you help one, you help all

Good people help others

If you think you are too small to make a difference, try sleeping in a closed room with a mosquito

To give and not to count the costs

Unconditional love

Generosity of spirit

By serving others you come closer to self-realisation, acceptance and ultimately peace

Love thy neighbour as thyself

How can I act in this moment in a way that uplifts me and others?

I'm here for something bigger than myself

What is the point of my life if it is only for me?

Within the overall human need to serve others we found two sub-themes. They are: **making a difference** and **meeting the needs of humanity and the planet**.

Making a difference

This sub-theme covers being able to improve things for others and can cover helping to improve people's experience of things, or assisting them to improve their conditions.

People in workshops spoke about making a difference in the following ways:

Giving back

Advocating for the needs of others

Helping others grow

Supporting colleagues in hard times

Challenging ideas that do not benefit employees

Speaking up

Examples of how people experienced this at work are: 'I know that the organisation is ever so slightly better off because I'm here'; 'I'm aware now that we provide work for a certain amount of people. To me that's very important'; and 'I used to feel that I could really assist our clients, now I no longer have time for that'.

Many sayings reinforce the universality and enduring relevance of this theme for human beings:

> Work if performed in the spirit of service is worship. (Baha'u'llah)

> We don't set out to save the world; we set out to wonder how other people are doing and to reflect on how our actions affect other people's hearts. (Pema Chödrön)

> We must not, in trying to think about how we can make a big difference, ignore the small daily difference we can make which, over time, add up to big differences that we often cannot foresee. (Marian Wright Edelman)

> Caring can be learned by all human beings, can be worked into the design of every life, meeting an individual need as well as a pervasive need in society. (Mary Catherine Bateson)

> Bad things happen because good people stand by and do nothing. (Edmund Burke—paraphrased)

> Let us not love in word, neither in tongue; but in deed and in truth. (John 3: 18)

And if we want to check out this aspect of meaningful work we can ask:

- Do I help others in my workplace?
- Do I feel that what I do makes a real difference?
- Are employees given the time and freedom to make a difference?
- Does the work we do make a difference to others?

Meeting the needs of humanity and the planet

This points to the need to be useful in the larger context, to feel that one's life and work have been useful to the wider cause, that it helps to meet the needs of wider groups, of the wider world, or of the planet itself. It differs from making a difference, where research participants referred to the elements of their work over which they had more immediate control and which were internal to the organisation.

People in workshops spoke about meeting the needs of humanity and the planet in the following ways:

Social action

Helping the poor and the unemployed

Sharing resources

Acting with future generations in mind

Having a universal consciousness

Giving back

Empowering the community

Examples of how people experienced this at work are: 'I work for a company that does good work'; 'We've just done this massive "vision thing" but our company makes no real contribution to human well-being'; 'Will it all be worthwhile if we destroy the planet as a result of our growth?'

Many sayings reinforce the universality and enduring relevance of this theme for human beings:

> For the sake of the welfare of all, carry on thy task in life.
> (Bhagavad Gita 3: 20)

> One thing I know: the only ones among you who will really be happy are those who will have sought and found how to serve. (Dr Albert Schweitzer)

> How wonderful it is that nobody need wait a single moment before starting to improve the world. (Anne Frank)

> Act as if what you do makes a difference. It does. (William James)

In the following words from Olive Schreiner we hear the longing to leave an enduring legacy to future generations so hauntingly expressed.

> I would like to say to the men and women of the genera-
> tions which will come after us. 'You will look back at us
> with astonishment. You will wonder at the passionate
> struggles that accomplished so little . . . at the truths we
> grasped at, but never could quite get our fingers round—
> but, what you will never know is how it was thinking of
> you and for you, that we struggled as we did . . . that it was
> in the thought of your larger realisation and fuller life that
> we found consolation for the futilities of our own'. (Olive
> Schreiner, *Women and Labour*, 1911)

We can hope that our work is a contribution, but if you want to
question how much your work contributes to the whole, you might
ask yourself:

- Do I contribute to products or services that enhance human
  well-being?

- Do we take the environment into consideration in all aspects
  of our work?

- Do we do work that matters or is worthwhile?

- Does the organisation stand for something that matters or is
  worthwhile?

Tensions between Doing and Being and between Self and Others

In the previous section we covered in detail the four pathways in
which people find meaning. However, meeting the needs of these
four pathways sets up **tensions**, and too much focus on one can lead
to a loss of meaning, as identified by our original research participants: 'I achieved a lot and am glad that I did it but had many stress-
ful times and felt my life was becoming totally unbalanced'; 'I just
can't get any time for myself. I don't spend the time properly caring
for myself.'

As the participants pointed out, meaning is found in working
through *all* pathways, and in how we balance or address fundamental

tensions. In our research we found two **tensions that relate to meaning**: one between **Being** and **Doing**, and the next between **Self** and **Others**.

Being and Doing

Being and Doing, as we have seen, highlights the need for us to move in some way between our human need to focus inward and reflect, and our need to act in the world.

Being focuses on the need to reflect. It covers such things as silence, patience, taking our time and thoughtful togetherness. It points to a need to be not only with one's self but also with others.

This too, is a universal and enduring theme:

> "" What is this life if, full of care, / We have no time to stand and stare? "" (W.H. Davies, 'Leisure')

> "" And when is there time to remember, to sift, to weigh, to estimate, to total? "" (Tillie Olsen)

Doing is Being in action; it is the outward expression of Being. It focuses out into the world. It is heard when we catch ourselves or others saying: 'I just can't wait to get my hands on that clay' or 'We've talked enough, let's get on with it' or 'I just want to get started right now'.

The need to act is a universal and enduring theme:

> "" A life of reaction is a life of slavery, intellectually and spiritually. One must fight for a life of action, not reaction. ""
> (Rita Mae Brown)

> "" What would life be if we had no courage to attempt anything? "" (Vincent van Gogh)

> "" Do you want to know who you are? Don't ask. Act! Action will delineate and define you. "" (Thomas Jefferson)

And if we want to check out this aspect of meaningful work and living we can ask:

• At work, do I often feel overwhelmed by the amount I have to do?

- In my work do I have the time and space to think? What is the effect of this on me and on my work?

- Would we make better decisions at work if we took more time to be thoughtful and reflect on what we are doing and why?

- At work do we have a good balance between focusing on getting things done and noticing how people are feeling?

Self and Others

The tension between Self and Others refers to the ongoing challenge of meeting the needs of the self, while also meeting the needs of others.

Self covers the overarching human need to develop and express our individual self.

Others reflects our need to make a difference and contribute in small and large ways so that we feel that our life has been worthwhile.

Keeping the balance between Self and Others is another universal and enduring theme in life:

> " If I am not for myself, who will be for me? But if I am only for myself, who am I? " (Rabbi Hillel)

We can see that meaning is found in the way we work with and through the apparently irreconcilable tensions between Being and Doing and Self and Others and that meaning is lost when one is expressed at the exclusion of the other. Tensions are part of the ongoing dynamic of creating a meaning life and meaningful work. By attending to them, noticing when they are becoming unbalanced for us (often signalled by strong feelings, upset or a noticeable loss of interest in something) we can examine and decide what to do to restore balance and therefore meaning. However, the challenge of balancing these tensions exists within the larger situation in which we find ourselves and make meaning. This is between inspiration and the reality of our self and our circumstances.

To check out this aspect of meaningful work we can ask:

- Do I often find myself resenting the demands of others?
- Can I easily speak from my point of view at work, or does the force of others, or the corporate culture, divorce me from myself?

Inspiration and Reality of Self and Circumstances

As outlined in the beginning of this chapter, here we focus on the bigger realm in which meaningfulness takes place, which is, at any time, somewhere between Inspiration and Reality; between our hopes, ideals and visions for the future and the place in which we currently find ourselves. We found that both were automatically made present in conversations about meaningfulness.

Inspiration

Meaningfulness is experienced when an individual feels aligned with some form of ideal that germinates from the human desire to continually improve oneself and to improve conditions for others. This could be drawn from religious sources, our relations with other people, strongly held principles or nature. Inspiration often includes the concept of grace and joy, a combination of outer animation and our inner response.

People in workshops spoke about Inspiration in the following ways:

Family

Love

My faith

The source of all life

The order that underpins the universe

Loving God

Following the vision in my heart

My will—God's will

Grace

The divine

Open to magic

Guidance

Divine love

Doors opening

Being aligned

Asking what is meant to be

An example of how people experienced this at work: 'We decided to start the meetings with prayers or any text that has inspired a person, and this focus at the beginning lifted us above ourselves.'

Writings from all over the world are full of examples of the importance of inspiration and here are some:

> The world is: all that there is. (Buddha)

> Just living is not enough. One must have sunshine, freedom, and a little flower. (Hans Christian Andersen)

> Grace means more than gifts. In grace something is transcended, once and for all overcome. Grace happens in spite of something; it happens in spite of separateness and alienation. Grace means that life is once again united with life, self is reconciled with self. Grace means accepting the abandoned one. Grace transforms fate into a meaningful vocation. It transforms guilt to trust and courage. The word grace has something triumphant in it. (Yrjö Kallinen)

> The capacity for hope is the most significant fact of life. It provides human beings with a sense of destination and the energy to get started. (Norman Cousin)

> You can't wait for inspiration. You have to go after it with a club. (Jack London)

> I keep my ideals, because in spite of everything I still believe that people are really good at heart. (Anne Frank)

      •• Hope is the thing with feathers / That perches in the soul, /
And sings the tune without the words / And never stops at all.••
(Emily Dickinson, *Complete Poems* 32)

Yet, though there is much written about inspiration, at times we feel anything but inspired. Here are some questions you might ask to check on how inspired you are feeling at work?

- Do I feel uplifted at work?

- Does my work make me feel hopeful about the future?

- Do I have a vision for my work?

- Do I experience a connection with the spirit at work?

Reality of Self and Circumstances

Meaningfulness cannot be experienced when we pretend, either in relation to ourselves or to our circumstances. It includes awareness that we are imperfect and live in an imperfect world. It can come from being able to discern the reality of what is happening in an organisation. It refers to a desire for authenticity and the truth, a need to be treated as adult.

People in workshops spoke about Reality of Self and Circumstances in the following ways:

Being genuine

Coming to grips with what is

A kite flies best against the wind

Breakdowns lead to breakthroughs

Disturbance and desire

When we are out of alignment with our authentic self, we experience dis-ease

Allow the ebb and flow

Real

Grounded

Not Pollyannaish

Grist to the mill

Genuine

Not pretending

Examples from the workplace are: 'There is nothing wrong with all of this mission and vision and values stuff in itself. However, if we are not allowed to articulate where we do not and cannot live up to this, it feels as if we mock something that is really quite profound'; 'When I read some of our ads, or value statements I think, "This is partly true"; this is a good company. But every time we overstate, we also lose a little of ourselves in the process. It has to be grounded.'

Again, the importance of facing reality is an enduring and universal theme for human beings:

> °° Weeds are so interwoven with the grain that we would, at the same time as ripping out the weeds, also remove the grain. Who wants to be without fault, rips out her passion and destroys with her weakness also her strength.°° (source unknown)

> °° Nothing but that which profiteth them can befall my loved ones.°° (Baha'u'llah)

> °° We cannot experience true community if we do not dare to ask difficult and pertinent questions. Similarly for employees it often provides a lot of freedom and creativity to articulate an unsolvable problem and for this to be recognised by leadership.°° (Willem de Liefde)

> °° The art of living lies less in eliminating our troubles than in growing with them.°° (Bernard M. Baruch)

> °° You mustn't be frightened if a sadness rises in front of you, larger than any you have ever seen; if an anxiety, like light and cloud-shadows, moves over your hands and over everything you do. You must realise that something is happening to you, that life has not forgotten you, that it holds you in its hand and will not let you fall.°° (Rainer Maria Rilke)

> °° To change one's life is not to change our outer circumstances: it is to change one's reactions.°° (Gurdjieff)

> ❝ When I hear somebody sigh, 'Life is hard,' I am always tempted to ask, 'Compared to what?' ❞ (Sydney J. Harris)

Sometimes it seems that we never stop facing reality, but at other times it is useful to check on how real we are being:

- Do we face up to reality at work, or is 'reality' all there is?

- Are we tolerant of being human?

- Do we recognise that life is messy and is that OK?

- At work, can we openly discuss when we do not live up to our values?

The dynamic dance between Inspiration and Reality too is a universal and ancient theme:

> ❝ To succeed in life, you need three things: a wishbone, a backbone and a funny bone. ❞ (Reba McIntyre)

> ❝ Reality can be beaten with enough imagination. ❞ (author unknown)

> ❝ Reality leaves a lot to the imagination. ❞ (John Lennon)

> ❝ The real voyage of discovery consists of not in seeking new landscapes but in having new eyes. ❞ (Marcel Proust)

> ❝ What we achieve inwardly will change outer reality. ❞ (Otto Rank)

> ❝ Reality is that which, when you stop believing in it, doesn't go away. ❞ (Philip K. Dick)

> ❝ No man will be found in whose mind airy notions do not sometimes tyrannize, and force him to hope or fear beyond the limits of sober probability. ❞ (Samuel Johnson)

> ❝ I have a very firm grasp on reality! I can reach out and strangle it any time! ❞ (author unknown)

Summary

In this chapter we have shown how the Holistic Development Model came into being, what its various elements mean and how they relate to each other. We have also shown how the elements of the model are not only supported by our research but also form enduring and universal themes in our quest to be fully human. To understand meaningfulness and its impact on us being human, it is useful to tease apart the strands that make up the whole, as we have done in this chapter. At the same time the different parts clearly relate to each other. In our experience it is how all these elements play out dynamically as we live our life that truly provides the experience of meaning. In the following chapters we show how the model can help us talk about and make decisions based on meaning and how we can take charge of meaning in our lives so that it can lead to an increased experience of meaningfulness.

Part 1
Taking personal responsibility for meaningful work

This part of the book helps you in your own search for meaning. Meaningful work and meaningful living demand commitment, being able to stand firmly in your own meaning and being able to stay in charge of it.

We start with the personal, because meaning is deeply personal. Only you can decide what makes your life worth living and what you will do to create meaning in your life and work. Only you know when an absence of meaning needs to be taken seriously. Only you can find the courage to live meaningfully and it is you who experiences the joy from doing so.

As we make clear in the second part of this book, organisations can and do play a significant role in the extent to which you are able to experience meaningful work. But in organisational life too we find that the first step towards collectively creating meaningful work begins with each individual worker reconnecting to what, for them, is meaningful. When we have a strong place to stand we can, from that place, make conscious and constructive decisions about what we want to commit to in our organisations, rather than going with the latest, the most convenient or the most pressing.

In organisations there are always changes, there are always choices that are convenient but not necessarily right in the long term and there are always urgent things to attend to. It is precisely because of this that we need to stand strong in what is important to us and take responsibility for it. It is true that some people have more power than others and that this might impact their ability to create meaningful work; it is also the case that it is easier to stay true to ourselves in some organisations than it is in others. This is dependent on the structure, culture and purpose of the organisation in which you find yourself.

We have, however, also seen time and again that those who become clear on what is meaningful to them, and learn how to speak about this with others, have been able to actively shape their work and lives to be more deeply meaningful. Your work reflects back to you who you are, the choices you have made, what you have settled for, what you are creating and what you are challenging, and what you rejoice in or have given up on. While work plays a part in shaping our destiny and takes place within large, complex and often seemingly intractable systems, it is also made up out of the daily choices that we make, and these choices create who we are becoming.

You may read this book for yourself or because you want to help others to work and live meaningfully. If you are, for example, a leader or consultant, teacher, or parent, we have found it is still important to apply the learning of this book to yourself first. Those who have internalised this work, who have filtered it through their own experience, apply it naturally to a wide range of situations and do so in a way that honours the innate equality in human relationships.

In this first part of the book we therefore look at what is meaningful to you and how you can strengthen and develop this.

The chapters in this section follow a pattern. We start by introducing an exercise so that you can experience for yourself how using the model can make a difference in your life. Next we write about our observations from working with the model. These observations include comments from workshop participants, colleagues and many others who have used the model over the past ten years and include helpful approaches to the search itself, ways of talking about it in different contexts such as family and community, tips to avoid getting sidetracked from the quest, and how to challenge ourselves while also being compassionate.

This section of each of the next chapters helps you to understand not only how to work with meaningful living and work for yourself, but also how to use the Holistic Development Model with others. We then connect our work to relevant insights from other writers to help you put your experience in context and enrich your understanding of a specific aspect of meaningfulness. You may find it useful when you use this work in groups and organisations to be able to refer to the ideas, theories and research that show its intellectual foundations and rigour.

3

Finding the words to talk about what matters

The big questions of What is the meaning of life? and What is its purpose? often seem too complex to engage with and too far removed from our daily reality. Yet it is in that daily reality, in the choices we make, and in the people and actions to which we pay attention, that we create a meaningful life. In order to create a strong connection between the big questions and our day-to-day realities we need a simple way of articulating to ourselves and others what is meaningful to us.

In this chapter we show how the Holistic Development Model can help us to put words to meaning, so that we can think and speak with clarity about the things we feel deeply and know are important to us. We also show how the model enables us to talk easily with others about meaning in a way that is grounded and easy to listen to and that draws out what others hold as meaningful in a way that can transcend the different perspectives and world-views that we bring to the table.

Making meaning visible to yourself

Let us begin with you, because it is important to first understand yourself and your relationship to meaning. To start, we invite you to work with the model in order to become more familiar with your own inner meanings and the ways you express these.

As described in Chapter 2, when you look at the Holistic Development Model, you will see that it's made up of four quadrants. We found these to be the four pathways through which people seek and find meaningfulness in their lives. We named them Developing the Inner Self, Unity with Others, Serving Others and Expressing full Potential. In Chapter 2 we described each of these pathways.

Exercise 3.1 is the first of many exercises that feature in the remaining chapters. You will find in Appendices 2 and 3 two versions of the Holistic Development Model. One has just the main elements named on it, while the other has just the structure and no words. We invite you to work with the version that seems best fitted to the exercise for you.

Exercise 3.1

► **Purpose**
To start finding your way into the world of meaning.

► **Instructions**
First, ask yourself, 'What did I do, or experience, in my work in the past week that was deeply meaningful to me?' (Check your diary if you need to remind yourself what you've been doing.)

Please write this down.

Now take a copy of the model (see Appendix 2 or 3) and write down your answers to these questions where you think they belong:

In Unity with others what did I experience that was meaningful to me? What was meaningful in Service to Others, Expressing Full Potential and Developing the Inner Self?

Doing Exercise 3.1 might help you recognise some of the pathways to meaningfulness that are present in your life but that you haven't noticed until now. You may see activities in a new light. For example, you might notice how a coffee with a colleague is not 'avoiding work' or even 'taking a well-earned break', but rather that it provides a real source of meaning for you both (Unity with Others). Or you may recall that in a certain situation you acted more courageously than you have before and that this is an expression of Developing the Inner Self. Simply allow yourself a little time to reflect on what you have noticed.

What we have learned

The importance of making meaning present to ourselves

One of the most valuable aspects of working with the model is that it helps people find words to talk about what is deeply important in their lives. As one participant said, 'We know when we have meaning and we know when we have lost it. It makes such a difference *to see it outside ourselves* and give it words, rather than just experience it as a feeling.'

We have found that words come quite readily to people once we focus on the four pathways. They help to break down the bigger questions into more accessible ones. These pathways are universal but they are also bounded and so make it easier to see how we live out meaning in our day-to-day lives, rather than trying to address more general questions about life's purpose. This focused approach helps us express what is important to us. This in turn enables us to more consciously take part in the process of meaning-making rather than abandoning it to others, or feeling inadequate when such topics are discussed. It helps us to see that meaning-making is a natural, everyday human activity, done by ordinary people just like us. It helps us understand that the profound is not necessarily abstract and complex but can be grounded and simple.

If meaning is so natural, why is it so hard to put into words?

In our research and work we consistently experience the profound engagement ordinary human beings have with meaning. This leads us to ask: If meaning is so natural to being human, and if it is often so strongly felt, why do we find it so hard to talk about? A fundamental answer seems to be that, while the search for meaning is intrinsic to being human, talking about it can be blocked by the approach we take to this enquiry. We are tempted to ask, What is the meaning of life? which can simply be too hard to answer.

One of the most well-known and -referenced theories on meaningful life is logotherapy, developed by Victor Frankl (Frankl 1963). His work arose from his experience in a concentration camp where he found that even in such terrible conditions the human being still has 'a will to meaning'. While this desire for meaningfulness is innate to being human, Frankl also proposed that it is futile to look for the meaning of life because the answer may well be impossible to find. He suggests that a more useful way of phrasing the question is, 'What does life expect from the individual, now, today and tomorrow?' Life, in this sense does not mean something vague, but something very real and concrete. The question of the meaningfulness of life is translated into more immediate questions of 'Why am I doing this? Why am I living my life this way, taking this path and not some other?' (Court 2004).

In our research we asked focused questions about a specific aspect of life, that of work. We asked, 'What is meaningful about your work, over the last ten years, the last week, today?' In engaging with these questions, people started to make finer and finer distinctions between where their work was meaningful, where work was neither here nor there and where it was demeaning. We found that when they were given this focused way of expressing personal meaning they often commented that they had 'known this all along' and experienced this reclaimed knowledge as being particularly powerful and fulfilling. As one of the research participants said, 'It is like coming home, coming to a very familiar, strong, safe and peaceful place'.

Coming home to ourselves

What we have noticed and are delighted by is that many people, when they first reconnect with their own meanings in working with the model, have this strong sense of coming home. Like any homecoming this can be emotional and sometimes a little uncomfortable, but also profound and empowering. People may cry, sometimes tears of joy, sadness or release, or from an insight into something they had been avoiding.

The model takes people back to the core of themselves, to their roots and to the things they know in their hearts, so they feel grounded inside themselves. The soul, 'the inner space in each of us', which has longed for us to return, feels complete. The deeper significance of this, as one colleague who regularly works with the model points out, is that

> In coming home to ourselves we also come home into the world. If we really belong, we belong in the world. But how can we claim and stand in our citizenship of the world without being at home in ourselves?

As everything speeds up we lose the ability to be close to ourselves and may no longer be grounded in what is important. It may also be hard to put boundaries between self and work and be discerning any more about what is happening to us as human beings. Working with the model helps us to hold strong to what we know. Having our feet on the ground of our own being and meanings allows us to more fully express our commitment, to ourselves, to others and to life.

Having an inner place to dwell provides continuity. Over time we can build a sense of permanence in ourselves where we can stand firm in relation to the emotions of others and ourselves, the changes that take place in our organisations and the things that challenge and frighten us. One workshop participant said:

> My job was radically re-engineered and during that time I stuck a copy of the model on the wall above my desk. It helped me to stay focused on what is important to me in the job and also to speak up if something that was important to me, such as having time to have a conversation with my clients, threatened to be engineered out of the window.

This sense of dwelling in a constant place can remain even when physically travelling, as in one case where a student reported that using the model while on an overseas secondment 'made me feel safe'.

Standing strong in your own language

Our ability to engage with meaning is helped or hindered by the words we and others use. Words are not neutral; the same word has different connotations for different people. To keep meaningfulness close to you (that is, to be strong in yourself while you engage with others), it is important that you use language that resonates with you.

You may have found that some of the labels for the four pathways are natural for you to use whereas others might sit less comfortably. For example, Unity with Others may work for you, or it may have connotations of conformity. Developing the Inner Self may not work for you because you believe that the self, or ego, must get out of the way rather than be developed. Some people replace Developing the Inner Self with 'becoming my true self' or 'developing my conscious self' or 'who I am'. In the next exercise we ask you to first ask yourself for each of the quadrants, Why is this important to me? and then, What do I believe about this? From there you can select the words that most accurately express your truths.

As you do this exercise, keep to the structure of the model and create a version that is based on the words that are close to your heart and that are based on your own beliefs. These can be from ancient wisdom, religious sayings, fridge magnets, family lore or anything else that has resonated enough for you to remember. As you can see from the examples in the exercise below, meaning may also be influenced by your current experience (e.g. I do not want to be washed away) or it may be a belief that you have carried with you for many years.

Exercise 3.2

> ► **Purpose**
>
> To own the Holistic Development Model and your own beliefs.
>
> ► **Instructions**
>
> Choose a copy of the Holistic Development Model (Appendix 2 or 3).
>
> In each of the four pathways, write down a phrase or two that sum up the meaning of this pathway to you. For example, here are some phrases that others have put in Developing the Inner Self:
>
> - You must be the change you want to see in the world
> - I need to know who I am in relation to the world
> - I do not want to be washed away by others
> - Getting to my true (higher) self
> - It is important to be conscious of what happens to my 'self' as a result of being engaged in my work
>
> Describe what's true for you in each of the four pathways and replace any labels in the model that you feel you need to change.
>
> Then go around the pathways and ask, What is the belief that underpins this for me? Write this down.
>
> At this point many people have found it helpful to create their version of the model that has our words on the inside and your beliefs on the outside (Appendix 2). Or you may put your words on the inside and then write up the beliefs you have that underpin these words on the outside of the model (Appendix 3).

People have sometimes noticed that, while they have plenty of phrases for one pathway, they struggle to find a phrase for another, or are dissatisfied with what they write down. For others, the permission to find the word that's 'right' for them releases a deep flow of meaning. Some find that voicing and claiming their individual meanings helps them overcome doubts about the validity of what they believe and gives them an increased certainty. In this sense the model can help us be the authors of our own view of the world, and therefore authorise ourselves. Each of us connects with every pathway in our unique way.

You'll also see that each of the statements in the example not only describes a pathway but also says something about an underpinning belief that you have. So you can begin to discern for yourself what you believe and connect this to your daily life. This can be done in your own words or you can connect it back to the writing of others or to your religious scriptures. For example, one person wrote, 'I believe that who I am becoming as a result of my work is as important as what I achieve', whereas another cited something he had once read: 'True loss is a life spent in ignorance of one's true self'. It is this underpinning belief that connects you to the pathway and, ultimately, commits you to living a meaningful life.

Since meanings are unique, no one else knows the meanings that are held by each individual. Therefore only we can uncover our own meanings and consciously claim them as our own. No one else can do this work. Giving words to things helps them become real and take shape, and giving words to meaning confronts us and helps us come to grips with what matters to us and what we believe.

What we have learned

Working with what we hold to be meaningful

Once we realise that we can quite easily speak about meaning, we can start to examine it. To own what we believe is meaningful is part of becoming fully aware as human beings and part of taking responsibility for ourselves.

Consciously exploring, questioning and examining, we can begin to pay attention to meaning and this helps us decide whether to keep, discard or alter meanings over time. For example, some time in the future if you find life a bit meaningless, you might wish to revisit Exercise 3.2 to check and possibly revitalise what might now have become hollow or formulaic phrases. Voicing our meanings, the things that make our life worth living, is an essential skill because it helps us to see that meaning is not just something that we find or that is waiting for us. A meaningful life is something we constantly create.

Once we consciously come home to what we have 'always known', our relationship to ourselves changes. There's a sense that what we have always known needs to be taken seriously and treated responsibly. We begin to take stock and can see where our world-views and beliefs have translated into action and where they have not. After doing Exercise 3.2 one woman said,

> What I see is that I've believed for years that Unity with others is really important for me, but what am I doing about it? Where do I find support? Where do I seek companionship? Just believing this is not enough. I need to put my beliefs into action, or it's all just words. I'm going to put the model up in the kitchen to remind me that the things I believe should guide my actions every day.

But while coming home to ourselves may increase our feeling of safety and solidity within, how safe does it feel to speak about meaning to other people? How does working with the model affect our shared experience of meaning?

Voicing meaning: changing the way we relate to each other

Margaret Wheatley (2002) writes that when we sit together and talk about what's important to us, we become alive. In this section we focus on making meaningfulness present in conversation. It does not matter which context you choose to first start using the model. The important point is to speak up about what is meaningful to us and also to learn to listen to others as 'meaning-full' beings in the sense that each person around us is also full of ideas about what makes his or her life worthwhile. It is particularly important if you are a facilitator or manager that you use the model with yourself before you use it 'on' others. This gives you a place of understanding from which to listen and speak.

Exercise 3.3

► **Purpose**

To practise deliberately bringing meaning into the conversation.

► **Instructions**

With another person—a friend, partner, colleague—place a copy of the model in a place (on the table, the couch or the wall) where you can both see it.

Take your time, go through each of the elements of the model and ask the other person, 'In Unity with Others, what have been some of your rewarding or enriching (use any word you like here but frame in a positive way) experiences over the last month (week, year)?'

You can make the exercise more specific if, for example, you want to evaluate a particular relationship. So, you may ask, 'In Unity with Others, what do you think we have done particularly well in our marriage/partnership, mother/daughter relationship, group or team over the past year? In Service to Others?' Go on around the remaining pathways.

Comments people made after doing this exercise included: 'It was a really good place to listen from, a place to stand for the richness and the possibility of the other person' and 'In evaluating our relationship from a profound place we realised how simple it was to actually talk about what is important to us, and how little time we do spend talking about what is important to us'. One person said,

> The deeper meanings gave us a creative place to plan from. For example, in Unity with others we identified that we had not been proactive in our social lives lately even though spending time with friends and family is really meaningful to us. So it was really easy to identify some actions starting with some simple phone calls to catch up.

What we have learned

If we are without ways of talking about meaning, meaning is simply removed from conversation. Of course we do talk about what is meaningful to us in our daily lives, we talk to our friends about our family's future goals, and we share stories about people we love. However, often these conversations take place in a private sphere, and we often do not think to ask, of if we do, do not know how to ask the other person what is deeply meaningful to them. The result is often that one of the most important parts of human experience is missing from public, and even private, discourse. Not only does the model help us make the inner world of meaning visible to ourselves, it gives us practical ways to own these meanings and share them with others. In addition, becoming more conscious and skilful in voicing meaning helps us create a variety of words and phrases so that we can choose how we speak about what matters to us and decide how open we want to be in professional situations, or where it stills feels risky to talk about meaning.

Practising speaking about meaning where it is comfortable for you

Once we are acquainted with our own life meanings and have learned to discuss these with a few intimate others in a safe context it might be time to venture out and find out how voicing meaning can affect group situations. This exercise can be used for any group, work team, voluntary group, organising committee or school board that is asking itself questions such as: What is it all for? What is our purpose here? What is at the foundation of our collective decision-making? How do we connect ourselves to the values of this organisation? or, How shall we plan for next year?

Exercise 3.4

► **Purpose**

To see the other as a 'meaning-full' human being.

► **Instructions**

Put eight sheets of paper around the room (on walls or any other place where they can be easily read).

Head each of these with one of the elements of the model: Service to Others, Inspiration, Reality of Self and Circumstances, Developing the Inner Self, Expressing Full Potential, Unity with Others, Being/Doing, Self/Others. We also provide an empty sheet in which people can add anything meaningful to them that is not adequately captured in the model.

Ask participants to go around the room and write down what they already *believe* about the importance of each of the elements of the model (You can also put this as 'what they hold dear' or 'already know' about the importance of each of the elements to them.) Make sure that they do not add their names to what they have written. Give examples such as 'In a previous exercise people wrote down under Developing the Inner Self such things as "you need to be the change you want to be in the world".' (There are many examples for all the pathways in Chapter 2.)

It's important that people feel free to write down anything that comes to mind. This can be wisdom from a parent, something they just know/believe, a religious text or a Yogi Berra quote, as long as it is meaningful to them.

Once everyone has written something down, ask the participants to go quietly around the room and read what everyone has written.

Then ask people to reflect individually on what they observed and, if they wish, to discuss this in pairs or as a group.

The first thing we have noticed when everyone is moving around the room is the respectful silence. As one of the participants said: 'There was a subtle change in the energy of the room as we started to see each other as "meaning-full" beings.'

Another participant said: 'Of course I knew that other people must also contemplate the meaning of life, but to so clearly and immediately see the evidence that I am not alone in this is deeply moving. The depth and breadth of all of the comments really struck me.'

In a team environment participants comment on how using the model enables and legitimises the topic of meaningfulness in the conversation:

> Having the model present, and being told that human beings know what is intrinsically meaningful to them, meant that I did not have to think about how my beliefs came across. I could simply write them down in the knowledge that others would do the same. It also did not feel too risky or self-revealing because the process allowed for a certain amount of anonymity.

Case study 3.1 is an example of what happened when one of the authors did Exercise 3.2 with a small group who have been meeting for a year to support each other. They knew of our work and had requested a session on the model.

Case study 3.1 Owning the model based on one's own language and beliefs

I did this exercise with a group of six people of varied ages and ethnicities who'd been meeting for a year to support each other. There was considerable trust and openness in the group. I went around each element of the model and asked people to write down the answers to the following questions: 'What is the key phrase that sums up why this is so important for you?' 'What do you believe about this?' I also reassured them that if they didn't have any immediate response it was fine to leave it blank, or just draw an image. At the end of the writing I went round the group asking them to read out, or talk about what they'd written, one pathway at a time. Each person spoke about what they put down and occasionally people asked a question or commented on what had been said. When we had covered all the elements of the model I invited a general discussion on what they had experienced.

Many were surprised by how swiftly they had responded to the questions, while one or two said they had struggled to find a phrase for one or other pathway. However, they found listening to the others' comments enriching and on occasion said, 'Can I borrow that? I really like it.' By the end of the session, which took about an hour, people were excited and moved. One young university student kept saying, 'It makes everything completely clear. I've only just discovered my spirituality and it was very vague and hazy. Now it's all clear. I can't believe how clear it is.' People commented on how good it was to share and listen to others. The variety of responses to each pathway enriched their understanding of the pathway as well as giving them deeper insight into each other.

What we have learned

Creating a grounded and safe space to talk about what's important

While in this case people were comfortable with each other, voicing our deepest life meanings in a group may at times be difficult. To make it easier we need to find a way that makes our inner self visible to others while at the same time not feeling too exposed or too confined by what others may think about us. It can help to bring our deepest knowing to the fore if we assume that many others share this desire.

The model, and the way that we work with it, does provide a neutral space where people can hear themselves and each other speak about meaning. At this very basic level, the model provides a place where meaning can simply be expressed and reflected on before people need to consider anything else. This alone has a profound effect on the energy in a room. Speaking or writing about meaning in the company of others reinforces for each person that living meaningful lives is important, even though for some it might be the first time that they have heard themselves speak about it.

The model makes speaking about meaning less frightening because, through its presence, it legitimises conversations about meaning. It puts meaningfulness 'out there' instead of just 'in here'. It makes our inner world more visible in a way that makes it safe because we are not alone. As one person said at the end of doing Exercise 3.4, looking around at his colleagues, 'I can't believe how much we have in common. Even though we expressed things quite differently, really most of us are saying the same sort of thing.' We have found similar effects with groups in which people did not previously know each other.

Shared meaning: identifying our commonalities, while also acknowledging our differences

Meaning is subjective. The significance we assign to something is dependent on the world-views we have and these vary widely. At the same time, in order to act collectively we need to connect and experience our similarities, shared in the very nature of being human, regardless of the differences that exist among individuals, cultures or groups. We have found that the model is an excellent tool for people to recognise and act on the commonalities as well as respect the differences of world-views.

Exercise 3.5

► Purpose

In this exercise we explore the very real differences that can arise when people share what is meaningful to them.

► Instructions

Continue with Exercise 3.4 and ask the people involved to look at the sheets on the wall and note the language that has been used.

What do they notice that they have in common? What is different?

Ask them to discuss what they observed, in pairs or in a small group.

If you did the exercise in a pair but are also intending to use it with a group you might also want to notice the difference in language that each of you used.

What we have learned

Noticing our similarities, while being safe enough to enjoy our differences

The Holistic Development Model helps us to connect at the deepest human level, because it helps to quickly identify the meanings on which we agree and to see where we differ.

In originally naming the parts of the model we deliberately chose words that are big enough for individuals to see where they connect. In other words, I might say 'teamwork' and you might say 'that's too much of a business word to me and I want to use "love" ', and a third person might say 'that is too touchy-feely for me and I would say it is about supporting each other'. The label Unity with Others was chosen because it captures in the broadest sense that some constructive form of relating to each other makes human experience meaningful.

As one of the workshop participants said:

> The model is relevant because people have beliefs about each element. It allows us to say, 'These are what we have in common and these are different'. The model helps us remind ourselves, when we get overwhelmed or frightened by people, that we in fact share purposes. It helps us to have strength and to stand for what we believe in.

While common purposes are identified, the model and the way we work with it makes it immediately obvious that when we move from the abstract to the concrete, people have very diverse world-views and experiences. Making world-views visible assists people to not assume that everyone has the same paradigm as them. For example, for the inner circle of Inspiration, one person might draw inspiration from God and another from nature, or ancestors, or have a word that captures all three, or none of these. People have in common that they need opportunities to be present to their source of inspiration, but the source itself is quite different.

The model makes both similarities and differences immediately present. This makes it easier to have conversations about differences without making anyone wrong and provides the possibility for enquiry, rather than getting stuck in dogma or just avoiding the issue. Neither does the model privilege one meaning over another. It therefore helps us learn to be skilful in holding to our view peacefully, staying constructive in the midst of contrasting world-views, remaining open to the possibility of change and creating space for those who do not wish to participate in conversations involving, for example, spirituality or religion. As one of the participants in our research said:

> The model allows the possibility of moving purpose from a purely individualised focus into a place where it is both shared and therefore collective, while also retaining an individual connection and expression. Because of this the model allows us to engage with the potentially divisive topic of meaning in ways that usually allow a greater recognition of what we have in common than what is different.

Identifying common purpose provides the basis for shared meaning and hence purposeful collective action that (because it is intimately linked to personal meaning and language) also engages the hearts of each individual. Another participant went on to say,

> Given that we can distinguish commonality it allows us to place this at the foundation of what we hold important and to hold to this as a group when challenged. Connectivity is stronger when there is an emotional bond so involving people—sharing meaning with people—creates a stronger bond.

On the basis of these deep meanings that have now been made visible, the group can decide what to do, and what to stop doing, in order to increase meaning.

Treating each other as meaningful human beings

The question of How do I live a meaningful life? is not separate from our relationships with others. The question does not only pose, What happens if I treat myself as a deeply meaningful being? but also, What happens if we treat each other as deeply meaningful beings? What if we treated our family members or colleagues as deeply meaningful beings? What if we treated those who are managed by us, or those who manage us, as meaningful human beings?

For example, having a systematic way of thinking and speaking about meaning enables us to listen for how meaning arises in the conversation of others and hear other people's meaning and purpose more distinctly. We are all used to hearing colleagues say, 'Why are they asking us to do this? It's entirely pointless.' Or, 'I've lost any spark of enthusiasm for this project'. Or, 'No one seems to appreciate my ideas'. These comments can often have the effect of intensifying our own sense of meaninglessness, but with an awareness of the model it is much easier to hear these as comments on an absence of meaning. We can respond more constructively and retain our own sense of meaningfulness in the face of these remarks rather than slide into a gripe session, as one long-term user of the model describes:

> I used to 'look for the good, or God' in people, which I still do, but having the model has helped me ground this. Now I also know that this person, whatever they are saying or doing, is also searching for meaning. It helps me feel a compassionate connection to them and listen practically to what they're saying with the model in mind. Often I can recognise an expression of longing for a deep alignment with others, or a frustration at not being able to express their full potential. At my best I can ask a well-framed question that can help them see a new way forward, but even listening like this makes a difference because it stops me from plummeting with them into negativity.

What others have written about the challenges and possibilities of voicing meaning in relationships

You might recognise just how much conversation about meaning is expressed in negative ways, as complaints, and see how holding the model as a framework can help you to steer negative comments into a much more creative outcome. You can also see just how significant meaning is in our daily and work life. At this point you might wonder why, if it is important to express and share what is meaningful to us, it's so hard to have a conversation about this, often even with those that we know relatively well.

'Human existence is in essence dialogical' (Frankl 1963). 'Human beings need and actively seek out dialogue and encounter with the world, with others and themselves. To this end, the individual and the world are inextricably linked' (Sykes 2007: 1,349). As we talk we construct the world we live in, and how we talk changes that world (Cooperrider and Whitney 2005). O'Reilley (1998) talks about listening each other's souls into existence.

This points to the power of shared speaking and listening as the way in which we both create our personal and collective reality as well as our individual sense of self. Once again we see the importance of talking about what is deeply significant to us because it is part of creating a meaningful reality for ourselves and others. It is important to find the support that comes from such conversations because we can often become isolated from each other and forget that a source of true contentment and well-being is simply to 'turn to each other' (Wheatley 2002).

At the same time the fact that speaking to meaning is difficult has always been recognised: 'There is a tendency to leave it [meaningfulness] unexplained or vague, as if everyone knows what it is but no one can put it into words' (Overell 2009: 5).

But Carl Rogers argues powerfully for the transformative power of what can happen between people when meaningfulness is voiced:

> If I can provide a certain type of relationship, the other person will discover within himself the capacity to use that relationship for growth, and change and personal development will occur . . . For a person's creative potential to be released, it is not the helper's authority, knowledge, technique, or interpretations that matter. It is the relationship itself that cures . . . Only by willing to be one's self within the relationship, by accepting one's own difference and having it accepted by another, can one discover the creativity and strength to change . . . At the foundation of human relations stands the ability to see each other as meaningful beings, to value the true humanity of each other. Not listen to each other as a technique of 'impression management' but as an empathic way of being present to the whole of the possibility of that person as a meaningful being (Rogers cited in Pauchant 1995: 202)

Voicing meaning to another clarifies, develops and enriches meaning, often for both parties or, if done in a group, for all involved. People long to have this sort of relationship with each other. People want to feel 'today I have brought the whole of myself to my work/relationship/club and the whole of me has been seen and heard'.

Understanding the vital role of meaning and being able to talk about it is an essential part of being able to have meaningful relationships. Given that we relate to things, people and events through their meaning for us, if we are detached from meaning, we are also detached from a constructive relationship. A 'take it or leave it' attitude is an example of this.

Martin Buber (1970) writes about the distinction between seeing people and their issues as I–It or I–Thou. In an I–It relationship, people are used as a goal, a tool for getting somewhere; people compete with each other for attention and become defined by their smallest selves. In the I–Thou relationship, concerns of time, space and cause are replaced by a concern for who the other really is as a human being. Buber writes that in essence this relationship is the most simple and mutual, because it preserves individual awareness and integrity while also seeing the other person as being wholly whole and purposeful. Of course the I–It and I–Thou ways of relating wax and wane during a day but the possibilities of I–Thou relationships are greatly enhanced by the ability to see each other as meaningful beings.

Our experience with the Holistic Development Model is that it greatly assists us to have what Martin Buber calls I–Thou relations and to sustain them over time. This offers something of real value in organisations where the general discourse has been hijacked by a neo-liberal and mechanistic world-view that has profound implications for our human ability to address issues of meaning at work. So, even when we practise bringing meaning into conversations and increase our confidence to talk about it with others, and our work confirms the vital importance of continuing to do so, it is still not easy to do in the current workplace.

Summary

In this chapter we looked at the importance of voicing meaning and how to do so to ourselves and to others. We discussed three ideas that are central to our ability to live meaningfully and where our research has found that the model makes a real difference in bringing meaning to our day-to-day conversations, decisions and actions

In order to live meaningfully we need to be able to put words to meaning. These words need to be precise and resonate with our deeply held beliefs and assumptions about life. Once we have these words we can think and speak with clarity about the things we feel deeply and know are important to us, and we can go on to examine and be responsible for our beliefs and the implications that arise from them.

If we want to live meaningfully we need to be able to effectively communicate what we hold deeply to others. We need to become skilled at talking easily with others about meaning in a way that is grounded and that makes it easy to listen to, and also be able to draw out what others hold as meaningful.

What we as humanity hold to be meaningful transcends the different perspectives and world-views that we might want to bring to the table. At the same time it is based on widely divergent spiritual and personal beliefs. As we have seen the model offers a valuable way to work safely with these issues. It allows for the possibility to meet and consult at a really deep level.

While being able to speak about meaning is essential, it is just the beginning. In the next chapter we go on to discuss how meaning is also found through creating balance and a sense of wholeness in our lives.

4

Wholeness and integration

The relationship between the elements of meaning

In the previous chapter we explored the importance of being able to give words to what we already 'know' and showed how this helps us come home to and stay strong in ourselves, recognise others as meaningful beings, have meaningful conversations and initiate meaningful action. We wrote that meaningfulness is found through engaging with all of the four pathways to meaning: Developing the Inner Self, Unity with Others, Expressing Our Full Potential and Serving Others.

In this chapter we discuss how the different pathways to meaning relate to each other. While this may sound complicated, it is something we are all familiar with and usually refer to as 'a balanced life'. Our research shows that in order to live meaningfully we need to pay attention not only to what we do but also to how the things we do relate to each other. We need to pay attention to the whole of our lives because when our lives are fragmented and unbalanced, over time we start to experience life as chaotic and meaningless.

As one participant put it, 'I got burned out because I was constantly meeting people's demands; a whole lot of people's demands and suddenly everything got very bleak and empty. I had no time for myself.'

We found that these feelings are very important to recognise because, if unattended to, they undermine the experience and process of meaningful living. Parker Palmer in *A Hidden Wholeness* notes that 'we are profoundly impatient of tensions' like these (Palmer 2004: 176). He points out that we dislike holding the tension of conflicting demands and want 'to get on with it', because holding tension can be uncomfortable and we fear it can make us look uncertain and indecisive. But how do we make sense of and choose between compelling and conflicting desires and needs?

Paying attention to the relationship between the pathways allows us to make sense of and work with our inner world—the home we have come back to—and organise it in meaningful ways. In this chapter we show how the Holistic Development Model provides a structure that allows us to do this. It enables us to organise what is most important to us yet is also intangible and therefore difficult to grasp and work with.

While we talk about the word 'balance', 'balanced living', as it is usually talked about in self-help books and magazines, can be too simplistic: it goes something like 'you need to decide on what life roles and activities are important or enjoyable to you and allocate the right amount of time to each of them and then "just do it" '. We have found however that the tensions involved in meaningfulness lie deeper and are more complex than this type of solution suggests. Our research shows that it is the nature of being human to experience constant tensions in our lives. We are not incompetent when we do not have balanced lives. We are experiencing the complexities of what it is to be human, and these complexities play themselves out in fundamental and ongoing tensions between the needs of Self and the needs of Others and our need for Being as well as Doing. In the model you will find these tensions depicted by arrows that simultaneously pull us in opposing directions. Managing these is a bit like walking, a dynamic process of balancing many aspects of movement without falling forwards or backwards.

Our first task is therefore to understand the role of these fundamental tensions in the human journey and to understand how they play out in our own lives. This helps us to notice our responses to them and any deep patterns and habits we may have formed. We discuss this in the first section of this chapter.

In the second section of this chapter we return to the four pathways as a very practical way to work with the tensions. While the broader tensions between Being and Doing and between Self and Others aid us in understanding and coming to grips with the deep patterns in our lives, the specific pathways in the model provide a very effective way of scanning for and attending to that which makes us feel whole. Rather than looking at the time we spend on different life roles, we can balance at a more fundamental level, identifying where we want to put our life force, even when life pulls us in many different directions at once. We give a number of examples of how you can do this, and how you can assist others in doing this. We then discuss the importance of working with a whole picture of meaningfulness for human beings: for example, in designing a work role or a training programme. As in the previous chapter, you will find a combination of exercises, ideas from others and practical case studies.

Recognising tensions as they play out in our lives

It has long been recognised that tensions form part of the basic fabric of our lives. Making sense of this phenomenon is an important part of the process of meaningful living. We may not always be able to resolve tensions but we can acknowledge and make sense of them, and learn to more consciously live and dance between them. In doing this we can also see and experience contradictions as opportunities for growth and renewal. Many of the great wisdom traditions describe tensions as fundamental to our human development and they are a recurring theme in the words of writers and poets. For example the poet Rainer Maria Rilke writes:

> Take your practiced powers and stretch them out
> Until they span the chasm between two
> Contradictions . . .
> ('As Once the Winged Energy of Delight')

Others have identified two basic tensions—between Being and Doing and between Self and Others—and noted how their relationship affects the extent to which we can find meaning in our lives. We begin with some of their comments. We then complete this section with an exercise in which you can identify how these tensions play out in your own life and provide examples from our research to show how other people experience them. In the second section we discuss how to increase our sense of wholeness in spite of inevitable contradictory desires. But before we begin there is just one question we want to discuss.

Is a balanced life a more meaningful life?

One of the questions that others have asked us, and we have asked ourselves, is whether we would draw the conclusion that a meaningful life is a balanced life. In itself, we would argue, balancing does not address questions of meaning. As Pozzi and Williams (1998: 65) put it: 'Imagine your epitaph to read "she led a balanced life".' On the other hand, it is really important to recognise that meaningfulness is found in many ways of Being and Doing, and we all have examples of those who wished they had spent more time enjoying their work rather than always pushing for the next rung on the ladder. Others talked about spending more time with family or in voluntary roles. In his commentaries on the writings of Gurdjieff and Ouspensky, Maurice Nicoll (1957: 326) says, 'To be balanced is not to be stupid but to be alive to every side of existence.' The point is that we can consciously choose to spend a great deal of time and energy in one direction to accomplish something that is special or important to us, such as running a marathon, fostering children or getting to the next step on the career ladder. However, when it is no longer a conscious choice, when we feel we have no other options, when we have not questioned whether it is still right for us, or when we go on for too long and exclude other 'sides' of existence that also enrich our lives, we lose meaningfulness. In the following sections we explore the tensions more fully.

The tensions between Being and Doing

An author who has written extensively on the tension between Being versus Doing in human life is Parker Palmer. He distinguishes the active life (Doing) and the contemplative life (Being) and suggests that contemplation and action can be felt to be paradoxical forces in our lives. He writes that they ought not to be at war with one another in us, but will be if we don't make conscious decisions about them or develop skilful ways of working with them.

> When we fail to hold the paradox together, when we abandon the creative tension between the two [the contemplative and the active life] then both ends fly apart into madness. Action flies off into frenzy—a frantic and even violent effort to impose one's will on the world, or at least to survive against the odds. Contemplation flies off into escapism—a flight from the world into a realm of false bliss. (Parker 1990: 15)

Both Being and Doing are features of our everyday lives. Our contemplation directs our action; our action in turn feeds back to us who we are and what we have set out to do in the world. Being conscious of both and seeing how they interact helps us to decide more deliberately how to use our time and what focus to bring to aspects of our lives at various times. Doing this can increase our sense of aliveness.

In relation to our careers, Marshall (1989), for example, writes that the very act of career planning can be very Doing-oriented. According to her, this type of career planning seeks control, certainty and predictability, is future and goal-oriented, and is about presenting the right image. Marshall writes that more Doing does not necessarily lead to better Being and questions the assumption that outward movement necessarily leads to inner development. For example, a new job or course of study really can help us to live more meaningfully, but quite often, after the honeymoon period is over, we also experience the same issues we had previously as old patterns reassert themselves. We need to become discerning about where we need to change our being, and where we need to take action.

In relation to the larger questions of life, Caproni (1997) expresses a concern about missing out on what *is*:

A strategic goal oriented approach to life assumes that
people have a great deal of control over their lives, despite
the fact that life is rich with unpredictability, problems are
often too big to control, and we are sometimes incapable
of and not interested in *doing* more or better. Joys and sor-
rows we never predicted enter our lives without warning,
and the blessings we have today may be gone tomorrow.
(Caproni 1997: 51, italics added)

How the tensions between Being and Doing play out in our own lives

Exercise 4.1

▶ **Purpose**

To explore the tensions between Being and Doing.

▶ **Instructions**

Go back and look at your response to Exercise 3.1 in Chapter
3. Now notice the amount that you have written down in the top
two quadrants (Unity with Others, Developing the Inner Self)
versus the bottom two. Look at how much time and energy you
spend on Being versus Doing.

Do you see a pattern? For example, do you see that you have
spent too little time Being or too little time Doing? Have a look at
a variety of life roles (parenting, community work, sport, etc.) and
see if you have followed a similar pattern. Where, for example,
could you simply be content with being part of something and
where did you need to direct things?

What has been the impact of this and on whom?

Is this a long standing pattern or a new experience for you as the
result of some shift in your life, such as retirement after a life of
focused work? How does this pattern affect various aspects of
your life, such as work, family, friends or leisure time?

As you reflect on these tensions, what becomes apparent?

In Exercise 4.1 most people notice that they do not have enough time to 'be'. Or that the way they are Being is not particularly meaningful. Some describe a pattern of running around and then collapsing in some sort of meaningless activity such as watching TV. One person grieved over the lack of time she has for meditation (Being) compared to the demands of work and family (Doing). And many others echo how they have ignored various forms of Being: simply being with friends, being in the garden or being present to what is. At the same time you may notice where you are developing skill at Being and the benefits you reap from this. One man who has always worked extremely hard was able to see that his forays into 'quiet time with myself so that I can ponder on whether or not there is anything more than this life' are becoming part of a natural balancing up of his overall life: 'I am slowly moving out of work and into this. It's scary, but it has its lovely moments.' This exercise helped him to understand more clearly the purposefulness of his actions as steps towards increasing meaningfulness.

Sometimes people also notice that they have spent a lot of time Being but very little on Doing or that there is too little relationship between their Being and their Doing: 'I noticed that I had had the same goal for a long time and that I was spending a lot of time daydreaming about it and discussing it with others. Yet after all this time I still had not done anything about it.' And: 'I know what to do about it, it's just that I keep postponing it, yet this not-doing is starting to take up way too much energy.' Often people find long-standing patterns:

> I was part of a range of communities and also, of course, of my family. Doing this exercise, I found that wherever I was, I was drawing responsibilities towards myself. I ended up being in charge of many things and enjoying few. I needed to learn to simply be with others and let others do more doing.

Another person realised that 'I am quite anxious about how the world works. I see I have developed a strong pattern of just being by myself or talking with close friends about what should be done, rather than risking real action.'

Taking the time to 'be' in our inner world allows us to explore it, to put what is inside 'out there' and so more easily understand and work with it. As one colleague said,

> People in the workshop could see their lives were unbalanced or that areas were unexplored and gained a sense of permission to focus their energy and questions in a different space in the model. It was very liberating for them and what is most important is that they have permission for making this shift.

What we have learned about the tension between Being and Doing

As we see in the last examples when they pay attention to tensions, people often uncover some deep-seated patterns in their lives. The following quote is from a research participant who, in her story, clearly identified the force of these patterns, in her case between Being and Doing:

> It has been a real battle with me regarding work because I felt my identity is so tied up with who I am in connection with my work; with the ability to earn a wage, with that recognition from the world. It is so goal-oriented and I want to become process-oriented, and I want to really let go and explore. Be more open, be more open to being able to respond in a more genuine way rather than what I perceived as a confined way, and I accept that being in employment does not necessarily mean that, it's just my experience of it and it's something that I see I need to address.

As we can see, these tensions are profound and not easily resolved. For example, overdeveloped 'goal orientation' can also affect other parts of our lives where we find we may spend much time Doing (e.g. running around attending various clubs and events) and little time Being (e.g. just sitting, sewing or reading, which are often times when our kids come to us with questions or just for a cuddle). The issues that arise from such profound tensions are complex. Here we can only touch lightly on some of the main themes with regard to rebalancing Being and Doing that arose as we listened to people's stories over the years.

The key themes can be seen to the extent we:

- Are still (within ourselves or in a place) compared with always being busy or moving

- Are fully in the present compared with focusing on the future or worrying about the past, or letting another year go by without being really aware of what it has brought us

- Learn from our being, notice our intuition and inner insights compared to ignoring or going against them

- Pause at the end of the day and acknowledge what we have in fact done (which is often much more than we take credit for), or work out what we can improve by simply doing something different the next day

- Notice that we have had the same insights for a long time now, but have failed to act upon them

- Notice that being present to others is the foundation of true listening

- Notice that simply being with others (e.g. during a work lunch) nourishes us

- Notice that having the time to be with others creates stronger bonds that serve as a foundation for collective action

Being has been described as the foundation of true joy and connection. Being still, reflecting, listening to the messages our body might give us, emptying out before we fill the cup again, trusting in whatever the universe brings us, being at peace in the here and now—all contribute to meaningful living.

At the same time we need to be aware of the future and actively create a future that we want. We need to be aware of mindless action but also notice when we hide from action because it feels too risky or demanding. We can both be and do, but to express both Being and Doing well requires us to remain conscious of the need for both, and to see how they interact and work together. The model simply keeps both present and hence increases our conscious awareness.

In this section we have touched on the tension of being and doing and commented on how we need to find a way to do both, although they often seem to be in opposition. In the next section we explore in a similar way the other fundamental tension, between self and others.

The tensions between Self and Others

As with the tension between Being and Doing, the tension between Self and Others is profound and has formed an ongoing theme in human experience and inquiry. In this brief account we simply wish to point out some of the ways that others have written about it and some of the ways that it is expressed in our lives so that you can easily recognise it, see it as part of the inherent structure that is the basis of a meaningful life and more resourcefully engage with it.

What others have thought about Self and Others

In what has been referred to as 'one of the most influential ideas in personality psychology today' (McAdams 1992: 340), Bakan (1966) introduces two concepts of 'agency' (Self) and 'communion' (Others), the tension between which he refers to as 'the basic duality of human existence'. Agency refers to the need for self-mastery, status, achievement and empowerment whereas communion refers to the need for love and friendship, dialogue, care and help, and community. Hermans and Hermans (1995), who developed a tool for analysing narrative in relation to counselling, described themes of agency as self-esteem, self-confidence, strength and pride and suggest that this way of being indicates that the self is experienced as an autonomous entity strong enough to cope with the situation at hand. It is therefore very important to us and not to be seen as selfishness but rather as a healthy way of being human. Communion ways of being are described by Hermans and Hermans (1995) as caring, love, tenderness and intimacy, and these terms indicate the experience of participating with someone or feeling close to someone or something. This other-direction too is therefore an essential part of being human. These themes of agency and communion are often seen as major organising principles in human life and as essential tensions that, if we do not attend to them, can cause our lives to become meaningless.

How the tensions between Self and Others may play out in our own lives

Exercise 4.2

▶ **Purpose**

To explore the tensions between Self and Others.

▶ **Instructions**

Take a filled-out copy of the model from a previous exercise.

If you haven't got a filled-out copy, take an empty version (Appendix 2 or 3) and consider where in the past year you might have had tensions between your own needs and those of others. This can be between different roles (e.g. at home and at work) or within one role, or a combination of both. Fill these in on the copy of the model if you wish.

Or you may do this as a simple percentage of the time you spent in one side compared with time spent in another.

Now consider the following questions. As an expression of tensions between Self and Others:

1. Notice how much you have written in the left-hand side (Developing the Inner Self, Expressing Full Potential) versus the right-hand side

2. Do you see long-standing patterns across a variety of roles of this tension? What has been the impact of this?

3. Is this a new experience for you as the result of some shift or current focus in your life (e.g. a new baby or a new job)?

What issues does this raise for you?

You may notice in doing Exercise 4.2 just how much time is spent caring for the needs of others, while your own are neglected. You may at this time, as with a new baby, be fine doing this, or you may, in terms of time spent increasingly at work or with your family, notice just how resentful you feel. You may notice that you spend a lot of time in Unity with Others, as part of a large family, but you may question the loss of personal expression as a result.

What we have learned about the tensions between Self and Others

Our research over the years shows some key recurring themes that emerge from the tension between Self and Others (Angyal 1965). Our intention is to just give you some ideas as to what to look for so you can better discern what is happening in your own life:

The tensions between uniqueness and belonging

People experience the excitement of being unique, independent and self-determining, of being responsible for themselves and having a strong sense of personal achievement and competence. At the same time they find deep and rich meaning in belonging to a group that shares values, interests and ways of doing things. But sometimes to belong (e.g. in a faith group) we may feel we have to suppress our own unique voice or accept that we bring only part of ourselves to a particular group (e.g. a sports club). Sometimes in order to stay true to our own unique talents (e.g. holding a highly individual view as an artist) we might need to accept feelings of loneliness and separation from others

The tensions between giving and receiving.

This is captured in the following story. 'Two years ago in my home town we set up a time bank. People offer skills and goods in exchange for someone else's skills and goods, without exchanging money. One of the unusual things noticed in the most recent evaluation of the time bank is that while most participants are very happy to give their time, they are very hesitant to ask others to do something for them.' This ultimately endangers the natural flow of giving and receiving, both of which make our lives meaningful. Another friend said recently, 'I just don't know how to receive'. Of course, some of you might also realise that the balance has recently been going too much the other way (e.g. your parents keep doing things for you and you don't have the time to reciprocate or even simply appreciate it).

The tension between taking responsibility and handing things over to a group

Here is an example of the way someone handled this tension. 'Recently someone told me about an incident at her school where parents were concerned about a matter. Her initial thought had been to take responsibility, take over and address the issue with the principal, but after some reflection on the right balance she decided to encourage the parents to gather and ask for their solutions.' In another example, a self-employed colleague without much paid work recently spent a lot of time working for a particular board she is on, because currently she has time to spare and others don't.

The tension of thinking for ourselves and accepting the wisdom of others

This tension centres on making decisions about which battles to fight, and which to let go; when to learn by listening and maybe see the limitations of our own point of view and when to hold to the importance of something we hold dear in the face of disagreement.

Summary: the effect of neglected tensions

The important point we make in this chapter is not that a meaningful life is a fully balanced life. However, if the balance between Being and Doing or between Self and Others is completely skewed for long periods of time, this can cause a sense of meaninglessness. In mapping out the time and energy you spend in each pathway, it is easy to understand why you may still experience a sense of meaninglessness even though your life is rich and full. Your energies might simply have been directed lopsidedly for too long.

Table 4.1 **Effects of extreme focus on limited pathways**

Developing the Inner Self	Unity with Others
Too *much* focus on this can lead to: • Passivity • Navel gazing • Not putting our insights into practice • Not letting insights drive our creativity and achievement • Ignoring the needs of others Too *little* focus on this can lead to: • Being washed away by others • Neglecting our own moral compass • Neglecting our own identity	Too *much* focus on this can lead to: • Abandoning the responsibility for developing our unique voice and contribution • Conforming even when it goes against what is important to us • Losing sight of who we are Too *little* focus on this can lead to: • Losing affinity and connection with others • Permanently rebelling because we can't fit in • Never getting the support that would allow us to contribute more fully
Expressing Full Potential	**Service to Others**
Too *much* focus on this can lead to: • Intense drive for personal success • Ruthless ambition • Disregard for others • Living in a world of our own and failing to contribute our gifts Too *little* focus on this can lead to: • Stifled self-expression • Inability to contribute our unique view • Failure to use and develop our unique talents • Becoming passive or even a victim in situations	Too *much* focus on this can lead to: • Martyrdom • Exhaustion • Or as Oscar Wilde so memorably put it, 'She lives for others, you can tell them by their hunted expression.' Too *little* focus on this can lead to: • Inability to give • Not recognising the opportunity to contribute

In Table 4.1 we have summed up the effects of too much, or too little, focus on the different pathways as a way to diagnose what might be occurring in your life or in the life of others. So, for example, you might be listening to a friend complaining that no one takes on board her ideas and see that this could be an inability to fit in with others and too full a focus on expressing her own point of view.

Using the Holistic Development Model to increase a sense of wholeness

From Table 4.1 we can see the way the Holistic Development Model helps us to quickly see what is happening in our inner lives. In the following section we go on to explore ways we can use the model to help us work constructively with the tensions between contradictory drives. We look at how we can move beyond fragmentation and make ourselves more whole and so experience a greater sense of harmony. We show that 'between the opposites lie all possibilities for growth' as Maurice Nicoll (1957: 239) says, and explore how we can learn to work with the differing needs in ourselves. The quest for meaning is a quest for coherence (Yalom 1980: 43). It asks how the different parts of the whole that is a human being actually fit together.

First we briefly show why it is so helpful to have a structure like the Holistic Development Model to help us understand our lives. Next we introduce an exercise that enables you to bring the different parts of yourself together and discuss what we have learned about living with all pathways in the model in right relation to each other. After this we look at how practitioners have used the model to assist others to create a greater sense of wholeness and the results of this.

Why is structure important to being whole?

As with all exploration, it can be very helpful to have a map to help us find our way. As we said in the first chapter, people often compare the Holistic Development Model to a compass, a GPS of the inner world, a map that links us to others and yet is unique.

The structure of the model allows us to find a way into the inner world of feelings, thoughts, beliefs and experiences, and then to systematically explore it in relation to living a meaningful life and having meaningful work. In saying this, one colleague points out that it is 'not like a blueprint. The model does not say what we should do, but rather gives us a structure to discern where we are in relation to meaning.' Another person put it this way,

> I say 'Never again!' on a daily basis, but you enter a corporate, and where's the space to move from where I used to be and don't want to be again? I need to stay in touch with my feelings. I need to hear stories, to listen. I need to check, am I falling back? We need to look after our humanity. The model is like a template I can use to check how I'm doing.

Structure, like a map, focuses attention, helps us to ask questions and look for answers in the right place. The four pathways provide a specific, yet complete, way of focusing. Rather than giving us the answers, it calls answers up out of us. Block (2008: 8) says, 'The word structure means to build, to construct, to form . . . It can be seen as . . . a quest not only for form but also for purpose, direction and continuity.' The Holistic Development Model is therefore not a substitute for who you are, nor is it a pathway by which to live. It simply makes visible what you already know so that you can give your life purpose, direction and continuity.

Seeing the parts in relation to the whole—and therefore becoming whole

To begin with we will use the four pathways to meaning as a way of observing our inner world and where we might create new possibilities for meaningful work and life.

Exercise 4.3

► **Purpose**

To notice the pathways of meaning in relation to each other. To look at a part and seeing how it relates to the whole.

► **Instructions**

Please go back to what you have written down for Exercise 3.1. Notice, as you look at what you have written:

- Are there pathways that are virtually empty?
- Were there pathways with which you struggled or felt uncomfortable?
- When you look at the model filled in, do you see certain ongoing imbalances?
- What else do you notice?

In doing Exercise 4.3, you might notice that some areas seem to be the full focus of your life, while others are empty. Seeing this helped some people understand the causes of discomfort or even suffering. For example, when, over a long period of time, they had only expressed Service to Others they now understood their burn out. One person who had spent too much time in Unity with Others began to see her conformity and question what fuller expression of her self could look like. Another person saw how bare Unity with Others was for him. He knew he was a loner, but for the first time saw an area of meaning that was empty and felt the sadness of it. At the same time, in identifying it through the exercise he began to see a way to address this vague depression that he had not clearly understood before.

For these people and others, there was a sense that meaningfulness had just expanded and that where they had been focused largely on one goal they now saw other areas that needed attention. For some people the different pathways bring up different emotions. In some cases people noticed that one area felt slightly uncomfortable for them and they didn't feel at ease in it. 'Oh, I don't want to go *there!*'

said one person looking at the quadrant of Service to Others. In her case, the word 'service' put her off, because of a family background in which women were supposed to be endlessly serving others. During the course of the workshop she examined how she might like to contribute, without the violent reaction in which her past experience trapped her.

The structure of the model allows us to see the whole picture while remaining aware of the elements that make up the totality of meaningfulness. In practical terms we need to make our peace in some way with the tensions of Being and Doing, Self and Others. It can be useful to work through the four pathways and examine these as places for potential solution. Since meaningfulness occurs through all four pathways, being able to see them all at the same time ensures that they all remain in our consciousness. We can examine one thing in relation to another, or others, while making sure we don't lose sight of the whole picture. And seeing the parts in relation to the whole allows us to *put* them in right relationship with each other. This helps explain why, after having been focused on a goal of Developing Self, such as getting a qualification, and having been totally satisfied, we may suddenly notice that the savour has somehow disappeared from our studies. Using the model we can see that our focus has been largely on Developing Self, and we can now explore the value in seeing how our work could be useful to others, how our newly developed self might now express itself in action in the world, or if there are others with whom we might share our learning.

The model is a way to notice the rhythmic flow of the tides in and out of different parts of life, and doing this can increase a sense of inner harmony where the parts work with each other and not against each other. To be whole, or working towards wholeness, is in itself healing.

In Case study 4.1 one of the founders of the Holistic Development Group, Patricia Greenhough, describes how she uses the model in her work as a neurolinguistic programming coach.

Case study 4.1 **The smallest intervention**

In 2002 I had a client whose father had died six weeks before. She said her mother had been very dependent on her father, that her father was a 'slave to her mother'. The role had been transferred to her and it wasn't working for her. This wasn't the only area of her life that wasn't the way she wanted it.

As a way to clarify just what was happening I explained the Holistic Development Model and asked her what percentage of her time she spent in each quadrant: '95% cent in Service to Others and 5% in expressing myself, which is all moaning about the 95% in Service to Others,' she said with a grin. (I do love the way the model can get right to the heart of the matter.)

The intervention was to task her to shift 1% of her time and energy from Service to Others to Developing Self and 1% into Unity with Others. She took a copy of the model home and put it on her refrigerator door.

Her mother died later that year and she told me that on the day of the funeral she noticed the model, still on the refrigerator door, and was astonished to realise that on this significant day she was approximately 25% in each quadrant.

I find as a coach, trainer and therapist that the smallest intervention that creates movement in the direction that a person wants to go in generally gets much better results than larger interventions.

Our experience echoes the example in Case study 4.1, which is that often people need to put only minimal increases into the impoverished areas to notice a marked change in how they feel. Another important point to note in this case study is that the solution is really constructive, because an absence or gap is clearly seen in an overall pattern of wholeness. This enables people to identify resources that they already have in more strongly developed pathways and to look at how they may transfer or link them to less developed areas and so address an issue faster and with confidence.

In Case study 4.2 a student used the model as a way of focusing her energies while on secondment.

Case study 4.2 **Consciously exploring the pathways**

During my recent secondment in the UK it was a great opportunity to apply the model. I was aware that there would automatically be a leaning towards the quadrant Unity with Others but I also wanted to spend some time ensuring that I am 'serving others'. Was finding balance hard? Was it possible to maintain equilibrium?

The first week of the placement was completely focused on connecting with the team, listening and getting to understand the dynamics of the crew. By the close of this period I was absolutely exhausted, fairly unnoticed and had gained little in the way of expanding my knowledge. So, though I had become part of the team, in some ways I felt personally unfulfilled. It was, however, important to try another quadrant of the model and, while I had the chance, I decided to see how balanced I felt when serving others. The mixture of being a trainee and focusing specifically on serving made me almost invisible at times. It wasn't until the end of the process that everyone made me feel valued and said I had done a great job and they would work with me again. The model had allowed me to assess the situation and which path I would like to take before I got there. It then enabled me to track my progress and assess where I was sitting, what I needed to work on and how balanced I felt at the end of each week.

In this example we can see that the student spent both weeks focused on the Others side of the model and that Self was feeling a little left out. At the same time, using two of the four pathways to meaning gave her a clear focus on the immediate steps she could take each week. She was in charge of what she was doing.

Making visible the different parts of meaningfulness and their relationship to each other therefore gives insights not only into the problems with balancing that we might have, but also into the opportunities we might explore and actions we might take. It does so from a profound, constructive place that is rich and non-judgemental.

Creating inner order: peace and consistency

Being able to see the whole gives us clarity. There is something about seeing the whole that is restful. We are not rushing around in an overwhelming complexity searching for answers, but looking at a totality and for our answers within it. Sometimes this can happen very quickly as in this story from Jan Lagas, an early participant in one of our workshops, in Case study 4.3.

Case study 4.3 **My journey with the model**

It happened in 2005! I was invited to participate in a weekend workshop with the model. I was aware of lots of spiritual influences active in my life. I was not conscious of which one belonged to what. My mind was chaotic in that respect. I had read about the model but never experienced it.

To begin with we moved from Developing the Inner Self to Unity with Others and during the workshops the things I learned landed. I was Being!

I became aware of the existing spirituality from the world itself. It is part of us, rooted in our very souls. The conscious thought emerged that all of us humans are capable of experiencing sadness at what is happening in the world. How we are all related and connected to this world and the universe in an organic way. All of this connects us all together. The question still is, how do we realise it?

In the next section I was pulled into the world of Service to others and Expressing full potential. In the end I realised it is all available in myself. I was Doing!

I am a religious person and I believe in my Maker. This weekend made me understand that we need a balance between the source of our origin and this world, our temporal place to be for approx 80 years. We have to learn to embrace our imperfections and not lose sight of our inspiration.

Wow, what an insight! The chaos subsided, the sky in my mind is clear and I know what I want to do more then ever before. At the end of the weekend we all had to physically express what we had gained. I literally made a mathematically precise dance, to show to myself and others, how everything was organically connected; the chaos was over.

Working with the model over time and seeing all parts in relation to each other brings about an inner order, and this is echoed by others who have worked with the model for years. As one person who has worked with the model for many years describes,

> I did keep saying to people that I was experiencing a sense of inner order, but it wasn't until someone else said that they experienced it too after years of working with the model that I began to take it seriously and wonder why this is. The model says these are the pathways to meaning human beings have for their lives. I began to order myself around them. Over time that ordering has proved to be sound. These pathways hold, as does the rest of the structure of the model. Sometimes alone and sometimes in conversation with others I find myself responding from the order of the model, with a quietness and confidence that I never had before. This inner order occurs from simply having the model as a frame of reference. I did not do a lot of exercises with it, but still found that over time I became more orderly inside. It works on me, rather than I have to work with it.

If we are able to see and work with the four pathways, all together, all at the same time, it helps us develop more consistency in ourselves. We can be a little more in charge of ourselves. Schumacher would say this is putting our inner house in order. Whereas Krishnamurti says in much of his writings on order that we need to be in inner order before we can create order in the external world (see, for example, Krishnamurti 1973: 306-17).

The impact of wholeness in our relationships with others

If we have an increasing sense of inner order, how will this—and our understanding of the Holistic Development Model—affect our relations with others? Often our response to others is a fragmented response. If we are not centred it is easy to respond only from parts of ourselves, to be easily swayed by dominant people, popular opinion and situations of unequal power. In these cases, without a strong sense of what is important to us, and a sense of consistency, we may respond negatively, block suggestions because we do not know why they don't 'feel right' to us, or just 'go with the flow' because we have nothing to help us argue another point of view. Or we can hear others struggling with conflicting inner drives and not know how to help them. Or we seize on one aspect of a conversation, neglect other aspects and leave with a feeling of dissatisfaction, as if somehow the conversation was not complete. In the next section we look at how relating to others from both a picture of wholeness and an increased awareness of wholeness in our self assists us to connect more deeply to others.

Listening to others with all the pathways to meaning in view

The first thing we began to notice was how working with the model began to shift our way of listening to people. We began to listen to others with all the pathways to meaning in view. For example, as we listened to someone talking about what they might need to be creative, we would also listen to what their creativity might contribute to a wider group, or with whom they could work to give fuller expression to their creativity, and we were able to ask more fruitful questions as a result.

We also found over time that staying aware of the model as others talk can help us to see a fuller person than we might have seen before. For example, working with young prison inmates, it altered how we were able to relate to them because it kept their human need to contribute in front of mind, even though, as teenagers in prison, this aspect of them might have otherwise been invisible to us—and to them. Acting as if contributing was something they 'naturally' wanted to do opened up very moving conversations about their longing to make a difference for their children.

In the situation with the prison inmates only one person has the structure of the model in mind, but it can be very powerful as a group process where everyone is working with it. The structure of the model allows for and invites reflection, and reflection allows us to gain distance. Questions of the meaning of life are moments of 'distancing' through stepping back and observing. While there are many processes used to create opportunities for reflection, the model is useful because it touches such depth, while retaining boundaries. The model makes the whole present to all members of the group. There can be a relief for a group when together they look at a simple yet profound model. They are not overwhelmed by complexity but are looking at a totality, and then together work on seeking answers within it. We will see the effect of this in case studies in later chapters.

Speaking from wholeness

Not only is it possible to listen to others from wholeness, but one consultant also describes how he used the model to speak from wholeness.

Case study 4.4 Speaking from and to the whole person

The indigenous people of New Zealand, the Maori, have a different view of the world from many Pakeha (the non-Maori people in New Zealand). As with many indigenous cultures, it is a view that is typically systemic and holistic. As a Pakeha working with a Maori group whose role is to provide a bridge between an essentially Pakeha system (a hospital) and the Maori users of the system, I really need to be able to understand and 'live into' this world-view.

When running a workshop with them recently I used the model as a way of introducing myself. I knew that I had to put more focus on Unity with Others. I couldn't ignore that they were Maori and relate to them as if they were Pakeha. So I had to openly and explicitly build unity with them and let them build unity with me, because relationship is so important within Maori culture.

Bearing this in mind I said, 'Ki te Ao Marama toku marae'—'Ao Marama (the name meaning "into the light" that we have given our house) is our spiritual home'. Then, in terms of expressing my full potential and being of service I went on to say 'Ki Te Ao Marama toku mahi'— 'Bringing things into the light, or throwing new light on things, is my work'. There was an immediate sense of rapport and understanding in the room.

Because I had come at it from the dimensions of the model, their experience was that their *mana* (dignity, pride and more) had been respected. Combining the model and *tikanga* Maori (the Maori way of doing things) made it even more powerful. I had moved towards them using correct language and protocol, but I also had a way of representing and expressing my fuller self. I now realise that I had been in the Developing the Inner Self quadrant during this entire experience; I had never spoken this way before! Using the model (I've got to the point where I cannot avoid using it) lets me operate as big me, rather than little me, as my biggest self, rather than my limited self. It gives me a language and a structure to do that and use it to also connect with the bigger them, their bigger selves.

Designing from wholeness

Part of living a meaningful life is that we address all pathways to meaning, and we have found the structure of the model is very useful in designing projects to do with human living and working. In Case study 4.5, one of us used the four pathways of the model as the structure for the design of a leadership course.

Case study 4.5 **Designing from the four pathways to meaning**

I was designing a leadership course for prison inmates and had begun originally by trying to get them to get a sense of their potential as leaders (while grounding this in reality and not fantasy). As I worked with them and thought about what would happen to them when they left prison I began to think how a course based on the four pathways would be a very sound structure and could help them to achieve more meaningful lives at some point. So I went on to design the following course outline. While the final three parts of this course did not go ahead for many and varied reasons, I have used the basic structure to design numerous workshops:

Developing the Inner Self

We began here, with a series of workshops looking at their sense of what leadership is, their experience of leadership, the challenges that leadership as a role makes on us as human beings, the possibility of all human beings being leaders and their own potential as leaders.

Unity with Others

Once they left prison, while they were still on probation, the goal was for them to find a community to which they felt they belonged and explore their sense of belonging, identify shared values and come to understand the needs and longings of these people. And how they might gain support from a community.

Service to Others

This involved them in defining a leadership project where they under-took to meet some need of their community and act as leader for that project. This section was designed as an action research project with plenty of opportunity for increasing self-knowledge while learning about the challenges of making something happen in a community.

Expressing Full Potential

This was the final part of the course, where they debriefed their lead-ership experience and began to see not only the challenges they faced personally but also to recognise what their unique gifts were and how these could be developed and used in the future.

In the final case study in this chapter we can see a wide range of aspects of the structural nature of the Holistic Development Model in play. Firstly in the design of their leadership journey, and secondly in the way it assisted many types of integration in the person who undertook that journey and in the business that he designed as a result.

Case study 4.6 Holistic leadership

The Holistic Development Model has a specific value in the area of spiritual inquiry.

Because of the framing of the original research and the focus on meaning and deeper purpose, and because, for many, the centre area of inspiration is directly linked to spiritual beliefs, the model can assist in an integration of spiritual beliefs and workplace reality.

This case study shows specifically how it is used by two consult-ants who wanted to develop a 'practical approach for opening up dialogue into the deeper territory around the personal spiritual founda-tions of leadership'. Both David Wetton, who works as a consultant at senior levels, and Sue Howard, who with David Welbourn wrote *The*

Spirit at Work Phenomenon (Howard and Welbourn 2004) about spirit-uality and how it relates to working life, felt that using the model could offer a deeper dimension to leadership coaching.

Sue first experienced the Holistic Development Model in a work-shop by Marjolein in 2006. Her experience of the workshop was to gain a greater understanding of the centrality of spirituality to a 'con-nected life' and to our leadership capacity. For her it was like coming home, and she saw that others, including sceptics, also found the workshop of great value.

One of the things that attracted Sue to the Holistic Development Model was the way it made it possible to link many differing per-sonal and leadership development approaches and so bring a sense of cohesion and completeness to leadership work. She felt that the model allowed people to get into a spiritual and psychological place in a way that is practical and grounded in the real world. In this sense it helps to show clearly the inner life and how that manifests in the outer world. So she and David Wetton, using the structure of the model as a base, created a series of eight sessions of individual spiritual mentor-ing. 'Our central offering is about developing individual leaders. We called our approach to leadership formation "Spirit(L)ed Journey", which offers soul friendship and mentoring to support the personal leadership journey.'

The model gave them a way to structure such a journey and provide cohesion within what can be a complex topic. The elements provided specific focus for a guided journey, but one that also left plenty of room for individuals to make their own discoveries. Sue and David agree that they would not have gone ahead with this project if they had not had the structure of the model to work with. The eight ses-sions allowed the person to go through each aspect of the model and reflect, with the support of both consultants and the resources pre-pared for each session.

Their first client, Jo, was at a crossroads in his life. He had the choice, in the challenging economic times of 2008, of staying with his firm or taking redundancy. He chose to step out and used the course to help him find a new way forward.

The eight sessions were set up as follows and the comments in ital-ics were made by the consultants at the time of each session.

Session One: Who am I? (Developing the Inner Self)

This provides the client with an opportunity to reflect on their life and share their story to this point. What is going well? Who are they becoming as a result of their life? What are their current leadership challenges and how effective are they in working through them? This session evokes a deeper awareness of personal identity, and increases clarity into choices that have been made and insights that have emerged. Hopes about future possibilities are surfaced.

> *In this session Jo was able to talk freely about his life story. We were blown away as Jo shared poetry, his experience of his father who was a healer, his own interest in healing, who he had been in the past before he left behind many things that inspired him, in order to get a job. This session had a great impact on Jo, as he heard himself talking about things he had not allowed to surface or express for two decades. And in doing so, finding that he was not alone and that he 'was not mad'.*

Session Two: What are my moral and spiritual values? (Inspiration)

This is a pivotal opportunity to explore what lies at the heart of the client. We enable them to explore afresh their moral and spiritual values and correlate these to their current work context. How well is the client able to express their moral and spiritual values? What is their lived experience of attempts to live from a place of inspiration in daily life?

> *In this session Jo worked through his values using an instrument developed by Cheryl Weir.[1] Although he had an idea of his values, this process and further reflection on the model were very revealing to him as he described what he felt about his values and how he experienced and expressed them in his life. He was left with an opportunity to put these values into practice in the new business he was developing.*

Session Three: Finding spiritual practices to nurture my workplace performance (Expressing Full Potential)

We invite the client to identify, explore and deepen personal spiritual practices that can support, inspire, strengthen and facilitate greater effectiveness in day-to-day business operations. These practices become an integral foundation to support the remaining sessions around personal leadership, being, as they are, a bedrock for spiritual awareness and growth. With such deep alignment a genuine sense of wisdom emerges.

---

1 www.cherylweir.com/bio.html.

This session was done at a church centre in London. As with each session, the Holistic Development Model was used at the beginning to reflect on what had been happening to Jo since the previous session. Jo was very enthusiastic and engaged, but we still felt that we had not got to the heart of things.

Session Four: Developing my spiritual character (Reality of Self and Circumstances)

It is without doubt that when one sets out on a course of noble action, such as an intention to live a more deeply aligned spiritual life, one will quickly come face to face with human frailty and failings! It is with this in mind that we help the client to gain clarity around weaknesses, inconsistencies and blind spots that may be tripping them up, providing opportunity for learning—and humility.

This session was held overnight in a monastery and coincided with a time when Jo was struggling to get funding for his projected website. It allowed him to question how he might stay resilient in the face of external challenges and in the dark night of the soul. Again the model was used as a tool for reflection, and Jo was able to share how difficult things were for him. We prayed together and Jo found it very helpful. It was a sort of breakthrough for him.

Interlude: Spiritual retreat

By now the client has travelled into some fairly difficult leadership territory. At this point, we advocate taking some extra space for time 'away' to take stock of the questions that have emerged since the outset, to find stillness and, perhaps for the first time, a deeper focus on what cultivating a spiritual life means.

Session Five: Standing on the shoulders of my spiritual giant. What is my ideal? (Inspiration)

Recalling individuals who have accomplished something noble and outstanding, the client is challenged to identify with a 'spiritual giant'. Insights into the character, spiritual motivation and life purpose of this figure leads naturally to an exploration of life purpose for the client. What is it that the client truly longs to do? Matching this longing with real-world possibilities creates a sense of breakthrough energy and passion.

In this session we focused on the ideal, Jo's spiritual giants, that is, the people who inspire him. In Jo's case these were mainly Martin Luther King and William Wilberforce (whose efforts resulted in the abolition of the slave trade in the UK) and what they had to overcome to reach his dream. It led to him writing down his personal vision and mission, which he found helpful.

Session Six: All my relationships are spiritual (Unity with Others)

When our relationships and related actions represent an authentic expression of who we really are, then a true sense of unity and connection spring up. In life, the most friction comes when our relationships are not in alignment with our deepest identity and values. We explore positive and not-so-positive relationships and how spiritual perspectives inform what can be done to build greater trust and alignment.

Jo loved singing and so we brought in a woman who taught singing exercises and we all enjoyed creating unity through singing. We then did a Quaker listening exercise, speaking when moved to do so, giving voice to the deeper parts of ourselves.

Session Seven: What difference do I want to make with my life? (Serving Others)

The penultimate session brings us to a wider sense of impact in the world. What will our legacy be? What contributions are we making to the world? How are we enriching the lives of those around us? Drawing together spiritual capacities, purposes and commitment for the long haul, we visualise with the client what the long-term effects could be if they truly lived life centred on their deepest inspiration.

This session turned from Jo as a leader to explore the organisation he was leading and how he was going to make a difference in the reality of that. Again, the timing of this was very useful. We covered service, Robert Greenleaf's concept of 'servant leadership',[2] purpose, vision, mission and values again. And Jo was able to think about these in a very practical way in relation to his new business.

---

2 See Greenleaf Center for Servant Leadership at www.greenleaf.org.

Session Eight: Reviewing and continuing my holistic spiritual journey as a way of life

Our work with clients leads to an empowered release. They have gained a greater sense of spiritual and self-awareness. They have experimented with spiritual practices and tools to help them stay focused and inspired. They have reviewed their life's work through the lens of making a real difference with and for others. This closing session supports the client to recognise the spiritual journey is a way of life. They may return to, and work around, the model as many times as they like to remember the holistic nature of living and the incredible importance of grounding life spiritually.

> *This session was a review and a celebration, which we were able to hold at St Mary Woolnoth in London where William Wilberforce received spiritual counselling [from its rector John Newton, a former slave-ship owner] that made him decide to take action on slavery. We stayed there for the lunchtime service and loved finding that a sense of spirituality could be encountered in the midst of the city. It's close to the memorial for the abolition of the transatlantic slave trade, which we visited afterwards. In drawing all this together, we again used the model as our foundation, our fundamental framing. For all of us it was very relaxed, a true celebration, a special moment.*

So how did this period of intense focus on all aspects of the model and this whole progress affect Jo? Nearly two years later we were able to talk to him about his experience. While he did not remember the sessions in such detail as they are recorded above, he described the process as 'genuinely life-changing, and in a way that was unique'. He went on to say:

> When I talk to others they say, 'Isn't it just a repackaging of business psychology?' I say, 'Absolutely not! It is an experiential process. It's like a hand reaching down inside you and pulling out the stuff that is in you that you mightn't want to look at. It's scary stuff. You don't want to face this deep stuff, but bringing it out, bringing it into the light, makes you see that it is part of real life and part of real normality.'

The process helped Jo to integrate what he had suppressed for 20 years and, in doing so, bring together

> two warring sides. I could see them as warring, even though they don't have to be, so therefore they were warring in me: spirituality and business, because business is all about profitability, competition, market share, and how can that sit with spirituality? But what I've done is to integrate them in my new business, and while I would not talk about it in

spiritual terms necessarily, and in many ways there's no need to, it is an integration of what I believe with what I'm doing.

The business is a social networking site, Good Connection (www.goodconnection.co.uk), and it's an example of a key belief I have, which is that we are human beings first, and that truly all things are interconnected, and we can't ignore this in our work. We have linked the social network idea with the idea of doing good, so while you are doing an everyday thing like talking with someone you love, you can be helping your charity—you can be benefiting someone else. This will begin to highlight that the by-product of our actions can be positive, and not negative—as in something like pollution. And in this way people can be allowed to express their divine essence.

Jo relates the way he thinks about the business to the elements of the model, especially the axis.

That doing something for the Self will automatically benefit Others. That in seeking Unity with Others (Being) we find ourselves (Doing) good. That in going about the daily tasks of our real lives, we can express our Inspiration through the choice of the organisation to which our donation goes. And when the website expands to offer well-being content (Developing Self) it will also serve others. It's a tangible example of no separation. As you help yourself, you help others—on earth as it is in heaven.

Jo has also found that this increased inner integrity helps him respond when people are in need.

Those moments where I'm really being myself tend to be when people ask something of me, when compassion is required. I don't have to think about it, the right words seem to be there. I don't think that would have happened without the course. It's no longer cerebral, I'm increasingly beginning to walk it.

These ideas have been with Jo all his life:

I did my thesis at Cass Business School, titled 'Man, Management and the 21st Century'—the title was a cover for an argument for business to change along the lines of recognising the true interconnectedness of all things. The work with Sue and David gave me confidence and enabled me to feel more relaxed about these ideas.

And put them into practice as the foundational vision for his new business.

The programme of Spirit(L)ed leadership journey supported Jo in developing this new business. 'I feel I am meant to be doing what I'm doing now. This is just the culmination of a lot of different threads. It makes sense of my life, which wasn't happening before.' While the course was based on the model and was used at each session, it was not just the model that created the profundity of Jo's experience:

Whoever is delivering it is critical and key. The model would be lost if the person delivering it doesn't fully appreciate it. Sue and David were amazing. If I'd done it on my own I think it would have limited my experience of the model.

Jo continues to support all of his development by using the outcomes from the course, reading more now and developing spiritual exercises. He considers the work he did with Sue and David 'priceless. If things go as they could, even if they don't, there's no way that it wouldn't have changed things for me for the better.'

Summary

In this chapter we looked at how the model assists us to recognise tensions in our lives and how to identify clear and profound actions to address issues of imbalance. Through the use of exercises and case studies we showed how we can learn to work from a position of wholeness or can design interventions with the whole in mind. The following are some key learnings to take away from this chapter:

- Having a structure, a map, helps us to understand where we are and therefore to make informed and conscious choices to do with meaningfulness

- Tensions between Self and Others and between Being and Doing will always be a part of meaningful living and meaningful work. Being able to understand them helps in making conscious choices about the energy we put into each over time

- Being able to keep all the pathways to meaning in view allows us to create more meaningful responses to situations in which we find ourselves

- Being able to express ourselves in all aspects of the meaning at the same time increases wholeness and, with it, consistency, purpose and peace

- Relating to others with the whole map of meaning in view enriches relationships

- Having a clear map to meaning allows us to use this as a fundamental approach to the design of many human activities, from a business to a course

5

Taking responsibility between Inspiration and Reality

When we can give words to what is meaningful (Chapter 3) and put different life meanings in right relation to each other (Chapter 4), our inherent capacity to live meaningfully starts to flow more naturally and more purposefully. In this chapter we focus on the next step, which is to bring this knowledge into action. Specifically we look at how we stay responsible for living meaningfully. There is a strong link between our ability to be responsible and our ability to live meaningfully: 'In a word, each man is questioned by life; and he can only answer to life by answering for his own life; to life he can only respond by being responsible' (Frankl 1963: 72). Buber (1970: 145) said, 'Every situation is new and demands a response that cannot be prepared beforehand. It demands nothing of what is past. It demands presence, responsibility; it demands you.'

We often know what is meaningful but struggle to align this knowledge with our actions. In this chapter, we explain that this is natural to being human because we do not take responsibility in a vacuum, but do so in the larger realm between Inspiration and Reality of Self and Circumstances and often bounce around quite wildly between these realms. We are all familiar with feeling inspired to do something but somehow not doing it (or not for very long). It is in fact difficult to feel inspired for longer periods of time and it is difficult to act on this inspiration in the face of our own shortcomings and the difficult circumstances of our lives. This, too, is a natural part of our search for meaning and many have written about how not only are we, as humans, not skilled at coming home to ourselves, we are also able to get completely lost:

> Again and again as I travel around I am stunned by how many citizens in our nation feel lost, feel bereft of a sense of direction, feel as though they cannot see where our journeys lead, that they cannot know where they are going. Many folks feel no sense of place. What they know, what they have is a sense of crisis, of impending doom. Even the old, the elders, who have lived from decade to decade and beyond say life is different in this time 'way strange' that our world today is a world of 'too much'—that this too muchness creates a wilderness of spirit, the everyday anguish that shapes the habits of being for those who are lost, wandering, searching. (hooks 2009: 1)

There are dangers in what bell hooks refers to as 'the habits of lostness'. Habits are what we fall back on if we do not consciously take charge of meaning, swaying between feelings of lostness and grabbing the first thing at hand that promises to relieve that 'lost' feeling. Individuals who do not succeed in creating meaning in their actions, relationships, or lives are often condemned to a state of boredom, discontent, impotence and existential frustration. This leads us to withdrawing from our responsibilities to ourselves and others (Frankl 1963).

Yet if anyone were to ask us, 'Do you think it is important that you take responsibility for your own well-being and that of others?' our reply would be 'Of course'. As human beings we know the importance of taking responsibility.

> The fate of the world hangs on the thread of our individual and collective consciousness. We may wrestle at times with the inflation and deflation that accompany such a responsibility, but to deny responsibility is to take flight from what the world asks of us. (Briskin 1998: 268)

In the original research it became quite clear early on that our quest for meaningfulness could be inspired by different sources and that it was helpful to articulate something that symbolised the ultimate purpose of our quest, an ideal towards which to always strive. At the same time, it became very clear that meaningfulness and pretence cannot dwell in the same heart. A space needed to be created where we could also face ourselves and our context as they truly are, with all their shortcomings.

When we deliberately stay present to both of these, it is much more likely that we can enact our dreams, hopes and visions for a meaningful life for ourselves and for others. Simply put, this is what the model allows us to do. In including both Inspiration and Reality of Self and Circumstances in the model it simply conveys that, as one of the research participants put it,

> Your life takes place between what inspires you and the circumstances of who you are as a person and of your environment. Be present to these, take these into account when you plan your future or evaluate your past, let these forces shape you into a responsible human being. Try not to do this by yourself but draw on inspiration and do not be disappointed when you are faced by challenges in yourself and in the world. All of this is a natural part of a richly meaningful life.

In Case study 4.6 in the previous chapter, we could see how Sue and David made both inspiration and what they referred to as 'the facing of human frailty and failings' a part of working with Jo. Jo got in touch with what inspired him and could create a vibrant vision to which he yearned to put practical hands and feet. At the same time, they did not leave it at that but asked Jo to face how difficult it was for him to stay resilient when confronted with the reality of his circumstances. It was at this point that Jo had a breakthrough and was able to work with these realities in a way that opened up new possibilities. Placing responsibility between Inspiration and Reality shifted responsibility from being a burden to being a place from which to experience increasing freedom and an ability to respond creatively.

In the big context of meaningful living the model thus reflects that we live between heaven and earth, or as Simone Weil so beautifully puts it 'between gravity and grace'. In working with the model we have learned that the way in which we position ourselves in relation to Inspiration and Reality significantly influences the extent to which a person can take responsibility for living meaningfully. In the next section we start by exploring the sources from which you do, or could, find your inspiration.

Inspiration

The central magnetising core of the Holistic Development Model is Inspiration, that which breathes life into, stimulates, animates and lifts us up. It refers to the human desire to ever improve, rise to greater heights. It is a place that sustains our will and determination. Some refer to it as a place of grace. Others as the place of hope, dreams, visions for the future and ideals—the field of possibilities. Each of these has been much written about, and they have in common that they focus on that which transcends our immediate experience. For example,

> It [hope] transcends the world that is immediately experienced and is anchored somewhere beyond its horizons. Hope in this deep sense is not the same as joy that things are going well, or the willingness to invest in enterprises that are obviously headed for early success, but rather the ability to work for something because it is good, not just because its stands a chance to succeed. Hope is definitely not the same thing as optimism. It is not the conviction that something will turn out well, but the certainty that something makes sense, regardless of how it turns out. It is hope, above all, which gives us the strength to live and continually try new things. (Havel 2004)

Inspiration is part of our humanness and we are surrounded with examples of the importance of inspiration in our lives through myths, fairy tales, books, the lives of inspiring people, inspirational art and music, etc. They are all examples of the human drive to aspire, to send oneself on a journey towards a transcendent goal. A 'sense of meaning involves some sort of quest' (Cottingham 2003: 33). If such aspirations are routinely dismissed there is little hope of bettering the condition of ourselves, humanity and the planet.

The model puts Inspiration at the centre, at the heart of our experience, acknowledging that it is the spark that ignites and nourishes our life, and that for many this is the core around which their life is centred. Inspiration sparks and feeds our energy, our drive, our passion and commitment and our will. It breathes life into the various pathways of meaning and pulls us towards them. Again, 'inspiration' may or may not be a helpful word to draw out the essence of what this element of the model is about for you. Over the years we have heard practitioners using many questions to get to the heart of Inspiration, for example, 'What is your well-spring?' which could lead to interesting questions about what causes it to flow freely and what dams it up. Another practitioner directs people to 'look for where you replenish'. Working with the model we can ask, What myth is guiding my life? What quest is my soul embarked upon? What destiny am I fulfilling? These questions enable people to quickly discern between what they think *should* drive their lives and what is truly going on.

Through Exercise 5.1 we invite you to examine your own relationship to this element of the model.

Exercise 5.1

▶ **Purpose**

To explore the source of your Inspiration.

▶ **Instructions**

Take a copy of the model and look at the central circle.

Ask yourself, What inspires you? (or use any of the questions above that work for you).

Write your answer in the centre and just see how it sits with you. You may wish to try out numerous words or phrases, or just stay with one.

Notice if this source of inspiration is surprising to you, or something that you easily recognise.

Notice if it is recent or has been constant.

Over the years people have used vastly different words and experiences to describe what inspires them. Here are some:

The mystery at the heart of everything

Seeking guidance, being open

Painting a picture of what's possible

The world, all there is

My children

The higher good of myself and others

Being with all that is created, nature, beauty, my family

Seeing suffering and knowing I must and can do something

My will —God's will—Grace

Being one with the Divine

Facing what needs to be done and just starting

Financial security

To do God's work

What you have written down may echo some of the above or be entirely your own. Doing Exercise 5.1, for some people it has been clear and certain. 'It's God that is at the centre of everything for me. Always has been and I imagine always will be. Nothing else makes any sense for me.' For others it was a surprise or a challenge to put a name to what they felt:

> I guess I fit into the 'pick and mix' brand of spirituality, seeking in so many faiths but without belonging to any specific one. I use terms such as 'God', but don't know that I believe in a 'God', just that it is a helpful term to signal what I'm talking about.

Or:

> I realised doing this exercise that really I have no answer, that life is a mystery, so somehow what is at the heart of everything for me is a Great Mystery. What was important for me was for the first time naming this, saying it,

beginning to wonder, 'Well, if it's all so mysterious, how does that guide my life?

Another woman commented, rather anxiously, that she had put 'anger' into the centre, 'because it is my anger and rage at what's going on that inspires me, is that all right?' We suggested she stick with what she had put down, and she went on to examine more fully this aspect of herself. Many people are inspired by their family or aspects of their work.

In doing or facilitating this exercise, it may be useful to ask more questions so that the meaning of the Inspiration we place in the centre can be fully examined: for example, What is it about God, family, nature that inspires me/you? It might draw out words that are simultaneously more precise and more universal and allow the person to dwell in the place of inspiration a bit longer. Or, in the case with the woman who put anger in the centre, it could be useful to ask, What is it that is outraged? What fundamental commitment is negated by the issues that make you angry?' Depending on the initial question you asked, you can continue along the same theme. For example, if you asked yourself, What replenishes me? you can also ask how empty or how full you are, what drains and what fills up your heart.

We have found that, if time and space permits, it can be helpful to send people outside into nature or, if this is not possible, to use techniques (visioning, meditation) or materials (art, poetry) to help people go deeper. What is at the centre is permanent for some people while for others it changes as they make shifts within themselves. It is important to stress that both are OK.

The question to keep foremost in doing this exercise is whether what is put at the centre is still very much alive. For example, one person reflected:

> At times I am trying to get closer to God and do God's bidding, so obviously God is at the centre. But at the moment that is not the case at all. The word 'God' does not really bring things alive for me at present; it is an automatic response but now seems too abstract. I need something more tangible.

Some people put down something very practical, such as 'success' or 'financial security', because many people have a very goal-oriented way of thinking about themselves and their lives. Asking more questions may help them see what lies behind these goals for them. For example, one person put 'success in my career' in the centre and then worked this out against the four pathways to see if this particular goal actually continued to be a real source of Inspiration. Once she had a richer understanding through testing it against the four pathways, she arrived at 'to keep my working life vibrant and apply it to worthwhile outcomes' as her source of Inspiration.

It can also be helpful to make a connection between this source of Inspiration and a specific aspect of work, such as leadership, innovation, meetings or client interactions, or to a specific aspect of family life. Again it is important to ask: 'And if you put this (the source of Inspiration) at the heart of your leadership/fatherhood what difference would it make for you? For others?' and so test this focus through the pathways to see if it remains meaningful.

If people are unsure about what is in the centre for them other questions might be helpful; Where *might* I/you get my Inspiration? How much Inspiration am I accessing? Where is it naturally present, where do I need to make an effort? One participant said:

> It shows us when the centre is weak and may not be providing enough inspiration because the model is like a gyroscope. The wobbliness of the edges—if you look at it as a 3-D model—makes it so important that we take time to really take the time to contact what inspires us at the core. You can really see why it is so important to have a strong core. It helps us to weather the storms.

Sometimes people have no immediate response to what is at the heart of things for them. It is important to allow them to take the time they need to work with this.

> When the model was up on the board my attention was grabbed by the centre of the model staring at me like a target on a dartboard. I found myself beginning a search not only for the missing words in that target but also for my own spirituality, something that I would have assured you was never part of my work. On the drawing this inner circle is a sun-like shape. For me this shape represents and looks like 'the light at the end of the tunnel', which gave me a huge sense of possibility and a small affirmation that

> I was making discoveries already. I could see the balance and felt the invitation to look through this tunnel and find the answers at the end. The search became about the middle circle and what needs to be placed in there to create this balance that the model demonstrates. At this point the word was most definitely 'hope'.

In *The Fifth Discipline*, Peter Senge (1997) writes that many adults have little sense of what truly inspires them. He writes that it is important to distinguish our immediate goals and objectives from the bigger purpose/vision/inspiration that is behind them so that we can remain open to the many ways in which that vision can be achieved. Peter Block (2003), in *The Answer to How is Yes*, explains that whereas goals focus on how to get somewhere, it is the 'why' questions that connect our whole being to the deeper purpose behind the goal.

At the same time we learned to work with what people put in the centre even when we might, at least initially, judge it as a limited goal rather than a transcendent vision.

> I had a client who put 'money' in the centre. I was surprised, and questioned her about this. However, she remained firm that for her money was at the centre. I became interested in why money was so important to her. She then reflected on the pathways in the model and reeled off the huge number of things she wanted to do with money (with others, for others, who she could become if she had money), which made me see things quite differently.

In such situations, bringing in the other elements of the Holistic Development Model, the four pathways and also the tensions, provides the person with tools to go deeper, to understand the why behind the how and thus, in this case, to understand their commitment to this goal by breaking the big question into smaller parts and then returning to the bigger questions of What is behind it all for me? or What drives it all for me? People draw on different inspirations at different times or in different contexts. We know of many people who keep their own version of the Holistic Development Model on an office wall and check in with it during the day. For them it is also important to know that the words are still alive. When you use the model for a longer period of time it is important to continue to question: Does this still hold true for me? Is this still life-giving, uplifting, vibrant? Asking questions like these is part of taking responsibility.

Reality of Self

The minute we aspire to something, the Reality of ourselves, including our abilities and also our flaws or imperfections, simply pops up. When we are inspired, we also need to learn to notice our personal response to the dynamic dance between Inspiration and Reality.

For example, one person noticed that she is a natural enthusiast. She can always see possibility in situations and relies on enthusiasm to keep her going. Of course, enthusiasm waxes and wanes, and she saw she gives up when the first wave of enthusiasm hits the challenges of Reality. Seeing this was helpful to her because it allowed her to look at what other qualities she needed in order to keep going with a project once the initial Inspiration had faded, and to sometimes be a little more wary of the ease with which she became inspired. It also helped her to enlist assistance earlier to address some real difficulties that the project faced.

It might be helpful to do another exercise that enables you or those you work with to better understand your, or their, relationship to the Inspiration–Reality dynamic.

Exercise 5.2

► **Purpose**
To see your relationship with the Reality of yourself.

► **Instructions**
Take a piece of paper and write down something that inspires you or that is a source of inspiration to you.

Now think what you have done with this inspiration to make it into a reality.

After a short time, shift your focus to how you now feel and examine for a moment how you relate to your accomplishment to this point.

Did you write down the small things you have already achieved or did you focus on the things you have not yet accomplished?

How do you feel about yourself?

What else do you observe?

In doing Exercise 5.2 you may become aware that over time you have a certain way of relating to the Reality of yourself. It can be particularly illuminating to see how you talk to yourself. Somewhere between 'this is just who I am, it will have to be good enough' and 'of course I can always improve myself, hold the possibility for a better me' is where a lot of our self-conversation take place. As one person said:

> I found it so helpful to do this exercise because I can now see how wildly I've been swinging between 'I'm great, I can do anything I put my mind to' and 'I'm small, what difference can I make?' In working with this part of the model I can now see that they are both true and that with that knowledge I can move steadily closer to what I'm trying to achieve.

You may recognise that you have a very limited conversation with yourself in which you first dwell on all the times you have fallen short. Or, you may notice that the way you treat the reality of yourself and others is quite supportive, or that it has changed over time with increasing awareness. Another person talked about 'valuing not knowing, being vulnerable, and surrendering' and is more compassionate with herself as a result. Notice how this self-talk affects your experience of increased or decreased meaningfulness. One person described this as 'the place of painful contradiction' and argued for the need to remain compassionate with our imperfections while not losing sight of the ideal. For example, in aspiring to live a spiritual life he says:

The model helps us to see how spirituality plays out in real life, how we are really engaging with it, rather than just talking about it all the time. Bringing both the ideal and the reality to the table is spirituality.

What we have learned about the relationship between Inspiration and Reality of Self

People have very different responses to when they face up to the Reality of Self. For some, the wise course is to decide what to work on: for example, trust or patience or inclusiveness. Some people make sudden changes as the result of a powerful insight. Yet for others it was simply permission-giving: 'so I am not perfect; well, I'm no longer going to wait for the perfect self to emerge, I'm just going to get on with it anyway'. For all of us there are times when the 'reality' of who we are may simply fall short of who we hoped we had become. Facing this, and articulating it precisely, became for some participants central to being more tolerant with the imperfections of other people as well as of themselves. Whatever insights we may gain, the model can help us work with our personal patterns and also help us to put things into place to plan for those unavoidable times when we lose touch with our Inspiration:

> I've always found it easy to be inspired, and easy to get stopped. I've done a lot of workshops and study and over the years become much more skilful at bringing a vision into reality, but working with the model over the past year I am just beginning to be able to take stock of myself in a new way. For the first time I can really examine the sources of my inspiration, to name these, to clearly see what is passing excitement and what is a lasting commitment. I have a much better understanding of just how hard it can be to make something happen the way you want it, so I don't underestimate what it will take. I'm still not skilful in working with others to make things happen, but at least I can now see this is an area for growth, and for the first time in my life I sense that I am unstoppable in the things I am fully committed to.

Another person talks of a star and a rudder: 'We need a star for guidance and direction and a rudder to help guide us in the current situation.' Facing the reality of ourselves forms a rudder, guiding us in the current circumstances, and it can also provide a clearer perspective on who we are and our relationship with the transcendent. 'Humility is being willing to be known for who you really are,' said one participant. And knowing who we are provides the real material for change. The more deeply grounded we are in our actual reality, the more possibility exists for actual change.

What we have also found in working with this aspect of the model is that there is a lot of laughter. 'What doesn't kill you, makes you strong', the saying goes; but it can make you laugh too. The humanity that comes into the room as we stare the reality of ourselves in the face also helps us stop obsessing and instead find things (and ourselves) funny. Humour is a key aspect of being human. It provides the release of tension in the rediscovery of common sense and common humanity.

It is important to find language that makes the losing and finding of inspiration neither right nor wrong. It is after all just part of the reality of being human, of being ourselves. Some people could acknowledge to themselves for the first time that they were no longer inspired, that the energy was sucked out of their work or lives because they no longer felt any Inspiration. It is hard to say 'I'm a teacher but I don't really care', or 'I'm a consultant and I get paid well for making very little difference', or 'I'm a mum, but I often find myself doing things out of duty rather than love'. It is really important to recognise the courage that making such statements requires.

At a recent presentation of the model, two nurses admitted that they were no longer at all inspired by their work and asked, 'But what are we to do? It's good money and we're both living on our own. We need to keep going as long as we can. We can't afford to notice that we no longer like our work.'

As facilitators we have sometimes felt tempted to suggest 'solutions', but working with the model helps us to support individuals to create their own meanings. As the facilitator who worked with the nurses said:

In the past, if two people came to me and said 'we've talked about inspiration in our work and actually feel we don't really care about it anymore', I would have probably tried to fix it. But through working with the model I could just go, 'yes, that is good to notice', knowing that on the way home they would chat together about this in the car and use the model to make some conscious decisions about it.

Reality of Circumstances

The Reality of our Self is, of course, not separate from the Reality of our Circumstances. And while it is true that we all look at the world through different eyes and have different responses to it, it is important to see our circumstances as outside us. In this way we can discern our responsibility in light of those circumstances. For example, for one person the reality of her circumstances really hit her when she looked at what inspired her: 'I like to think that I do this work to help people see the possibilities of life even when they are often very sick, but in reality I am not working from that energy, I am stuck in paperwork and meetings.'

Here, through working with the model, she recognised that her circumstances have changed to the extent that work that previously was meaningful, and that she still feels should be meaningful, has in fact turned into a series of meaningless bureaucratic tasks.

In this section we explore a range of responses people have to the Reality of their Circumstances. But we will begin with Exercise 5.3 for you to explore your own response to the Reality of your Circumstances.

Exercise 5.3

► **Purpose**

To explore the impact of circumstances on your Inspiration.

► **Instructions**

Looking back at Exercises 5.1 and 5.2, notice how your circumstances play a part in whether or not you are able to maintain connection with your inspiration.

Make sure that you carefully note all circumstances that affect your situation. Try not to self-censure at this point, e.g. don't go 'oh, that is not really a big deal'; just write it all down.

Is there one specific circumstance that challenges you, or does it 'all just seem too hard'?

What ways do you have to support yourself in keeping going?

What continues to defeat you?

The first thing that we often notice when we ask people to describe their 'circumstances' is that some self-editing takes place. 'Surely, this is only a small thing, others have it much worse.' For example, as we are writing this book during the recent earthquakes in Christchurch, New Zealand, we notice how people have found it really hard to accept their grief about a wall that came down and destroyed their garden, or broken family heirlooms, because 'others have lost everything'. Of course it is good to see things in perspective, but it is also good to accept what you feel and how that might result in a loss of meaning. For example, the heirlooms might be precious because they connected you to your family. It is difficult to understand our responses to circumstances if our real feelings are not properly acknowledged. We noticed how, when we asked people to describe their circumstances at work, it was often the first time that they gave themselves permission to consider how some of these circumstances had actually stripped away a lot of meaning from their lives.

Another thing we noticed is that facing circumstances can release enormous energy. For example, after the earthquake, we heard of a man who, overnight, became an inspired builder of outside toilets.

Another example is the man whose very funny online writing enabled him to successfully auction off for charity a boulder that had gone through his house. One woman immediately started to collect aid in her own town, drove overnight to the city, identified the poorest suburb and went to work knocking on elderly people's doors, finding many without food, water or power, some still cowering under beds and tables. This woman watched the same news as so many did that night, and many others have the skills she has, but she allowed the circumstances to enter her heart and responded because, as she felt 'there really was no other choice'.

In facing your circumstances, you may notice that you have become resigned, even despairing about things and feel overwhelmed or lost in some way. Or you may see that you over the years you have become more robust and resilient and have some good coping strategies. You may find your current circumstances quite exhilarating and that things have never been better. You may notice how circumstances such as health, a boss, a relationship (or lack of it), family circumstances or even the evening news can impact on how you feel. We all have different ways of making sense of our circumstances. One person talks about 'allowing the ebb and flow of life' as a way of being with the events that life brings; another says, 'The universe keeps bringing us the same lessons, until we learn them.' Circumstances can crush people and be too brutal and overwhelming. Reality can be the graveyard of dreams, aspirations, longing and hope. And yet reality can offer such benefits. It can strip us to the bone and reshape and purify us in some way, making us humble, strong and compassionate. Some are inspired by circumstances; they are the making of them. They see poverty and do what they can to eradicate it; experience hardship and become determined that the same must not happen to others. Each of us responds to circumstances in our own way.

In Case study 5.1 we see how once we can objectively work with our circumstances we can more easily reconnect with what inspires us – even when the circumstances remain largely the same.

Case study 5.1 **Finding Inspiration in Reality**

I had been telling the same story about my workplace for a while. I would have conversations with others at work about the bad decision-making and how it sucked the energy from me. Of course, I would pick my battles and challenge some of this, but overall, work was increasingly draining my energy. One evening I was talking to a friend who works with the model. She asked me to list all the things in my work circumstances that depleted my life-force. I arrived at the following list:

- I spend less time with the children and more with the parents
- Because of new safety regulations the extra-curricular activities that I would enjoy and volunteer for, such as tramping, have been cut
- We have gone to a new roster, which means my breaks always coincide with minding children in the playground
- Meeting times had moved to after school times, often conflicting with the needs of my own young family

What I noticed was that the list was pretty big. What I also noticed was that all of these things were true; I had not written down anything that was not real.

Contrary to my expectations, facing my 'list of woes' did not make me feel depressed. It made me realise how many distractions there were to what I inherently love to do: teach the children. It also made me realise that in each of the elements of the model there were circumstances that made it harder to experience those rich meanings. For example, in Unity with Others I no longer got to spend as much time with fellow teachers and parents during the tramps, in Self and Other I had hardly any time to myself during the day because of the way the breaks were now scheduled and I already have a job that is very Other-oriented. In Developing Full Potential I had been letting go of professional development opportunities because they just seemed another thing on my list of things to do. This exercise made me realise that I had lost many things that were meaningful to me and that my circumstances had really changed.

My first reaction was to draw up a list with things in my circumstances (or context) that I really liked. That was helpful because it allowed me to see reality as it truly was, with all the positive things that I still really liked about my job.

Now that I had mapped all circumstances, it also raised the question, What are you going to do in response to these? I divided them up into things I did control and things I could not control. Some things that I had challenged before became clearer and so now I could put forward a clearer argument. For example, I again challenged the lunch breaks, explaining that I needed some time in the day to reflect and evaluate and that this was central to my professional well-being and the quality of my teaching. This time I was heard. We came up with a new roster that allowed me to take those breaks at least three times a week. Other issues I still could not change but I could change my position on them once I understood why they were so important to me. For example, I realised that I needed to replace the tramps with something else that included colleagues and parents and arrived at a different physical activity that included both. Some things, such as the amount of time parents took up, I could more proactively put some boundaries around in a way that the parents understood by explaining that I needed most of my energies to go to the kids. Some things I could make more conscious choices about, such as picking one professional development activity that felt light or fun or energising. Some things, such as the meeting times, I couldn't change and it clarified that I needed to draw on additional help at home for a few hours a week.

Doing this exercise helped me to do three things:

1. My discontent changed from 'a feeling' to something I could clearly see and hence actively manage. I no longer felt impotent even though there were still many times when I could not change my circumstances

2. I could better place myself in relation to my circumstances. I could more clearly see 'this is what I can control and this is where I can create more meaningful work', 'this is what I cannot control and where I can work more actively to not get lost in my circumstances, to not let them erode my love for my job'

3. I could decide better how I wanted to be with others in relation to our shared circumstances. For example, I realised that while at first it was good to talk to colleagues about things that didn't work for us, having the same conversations over and over again also felt powerless and dispiriting. I'm working at ways we can still face our shared reality but also talk to each other in ways that are encouraging and appreciative

Working between Inspiration and Reality

In our research we found that people reported that just by itself Inspiration can become unstuck or ungrounded. If we only dwell in the field of Inspiration we may become too Pollyannaish, or escape into fantasy or delusion. Inspiration therefore needs to stand in relation to Reality. Reality refers to both the reality of ourselves, which we can always develop in some way, and the reality of our circumstances—the context in which we and our organisations find ourselves—which are also open to improvement. We will always battle with imperfection and constraints. Anselm Gruen (1999) suggests that the Latin word *humilitas* has at its root *humus*, the earth. Humility is befriending our earthly gravity, the world of our instincts, material demands or needs, and shadow sides. Humility is therefore the courage to see reality.

When we embrace our earthliness we often also get a clearer perspective on who we are and our relationship with the transcendent.

It was surprising how often the need to feel grounded arose as a core part of our conversations about meaningfulness at work:

> There is nothing wrong with all of this mission and vision and values stuff itself. However, if we are not allowed to articulate where we do not and cannot live up to this, it feels as if we mock something that is really quite profound.

Whereas many commented it was a great relief and that it grounded their work when they saw a model (and way of working) that squarely addressed their sense that life is hard and used terms such as 'facing imperfections', some felt it needed to be positively framed, for example, as 'opportunities to learn'. But others felt this would be too prescriptive, in that meaningfulness also came from having the freedom to just face what is without immediately framing possible solutions.

Ten years of research found that meaning takes place between the ideal we strive for and the facing of what is, and that once this is recognised people can make conscious responses to both Inspiration and Reality of Self and Circumstances. How they make these choices is up to them but it is important to allow time to grasp the enormity (and simplicity) of the interaction between Inspiration and Reality of Self and Circumstances as the theatre of meaning-making.

Between Inspiration and Reality, between possibility and failure, between idea, ideal, vision and actuality, is where the human experience takes place. It is between these two aspects of our lives that we experience the challenge and essence of living, of being human. In this sense what the model offers is a clear picture of the field of our human experience. Once again it simply makes visible what is already known and experienced by us all. And once again it helps us actively engage with and examine the dynamic relationship between Inspiration and Reality and our ability to live meaningfully.

Summary

In this chapter we addressed the relationship between Inspiration and Reality at a personal level. The presence of Inspiration *and* Reality of Self and Circumstances in the model offers something that is very simple and very profound. The human being cries out for a way of making sense of our lives that tells us that we are more than our concerns, our roles or our interests. Our ability to elevate ourselves can be inspired in numerous ways and we presented exercises that aided you to get in touch with what inspires you. At the same time we are imperfect human beings who function in an environment that presents numerous challenges to our ideals. The importance of making both of these present, as the model does, is that:

- The model is true to life as we experience it

- We can check our own relationship with inspiration and reality and distinguish unhealthy, discouraging or paralysing ways of engaging with them as well as encouraging, vibrant and life-giving ways of taking responsibility and creating meaningful lives

- We can take reality into account when we are taking action on inspiration so that we will not give up or be disappointed.

And we know where to find the inspiration to stay responsible in spite of setbacks

In the previous three chapters we have looked at how we can give words to meaning, put different life meanings in constructive relation to each other and take responsibility for living meaningfully. In the next section we discuss the relevance of these to organisational practice and design.

Part 2
Where meaning meets organisation

Organisations have powerful influence over the extent to which we can be fully human and can pursue meaningfulness. At the same time, our ability to get and remain in touch with our humanity is a powerful motivational force and can substantially influence the organisations in which we are employed. Our aim in Part 2 is to show how the model can assist us as employees, managers and leaders to rise above the immediate demands that organisational life places upon us. We show how having the model at your fingertips at any time and in any situation enables you to clearly work out what action best suits the higher purpose you have for your role, your people and your organisation.

Recently a document was brought to our attention by one of our colleagues. It was a set of instructions for the implementation of a revised IT system. It mentioned the usual implementation strategies, time-lines, etc. However, what struck our colleague was that, in handwriting, at the top of the document the CEO had written 'Above all do not forget that the people who are to be using this system are human beings'.

In pointing out the humanity of the people using the IT system the CEO may have intended to keep visible something that is daily lost in the workplace. When we forget our humanness in our organisational thinking and planning we are in danger of dehumanising our workplaces and therefore unconsciously removing meaning from much of our work.

And while it is charming to hear about a CEO who points out that there are human beings at work in this organisation, how would it have been received if someone in a lower position in the organisation had raised this? How would it have been heard, and what difference would it have made, if one of the 'end-users' had pointed out that they were human beings and that what was being implemented, or how it was done, diminished their humanity in some way? How would they have voiced this in a way that it could be heard? Would it have worked for them to simply say (as people in organisations so often do) 'I don't understand the point of this change?'

A less generous interpretation of the CEO's communication might suggest he was warning the implementers that they would have to deal with human beings who might make things difficult. Do those higher up in the organisation expect human beings to get in the way? And, if so, what exactly gets in the way of what? This issue has long been documented. Henry Ford asked, 'Why do I always have to deal with the whole person when all I want is a pair of hands'? Anita Roddick noted more than a century later, 'We advertised for employees but we found that people turned up instead'. And if people are seen as a nuisance at work, then what happens to the meaning that is of such importance to us?

Organisations are paradoxical. On the one hand, they organise their practices on the assumption that what intrinsically motivates and engages employees is central to the success of the organisation. They need engaged people at work, who can give their best to the organisation. On the other hand, with their relentless focus on productivity and efficiency, organisations are extremely challenging contexts in which to work and live meaningfully.

Organisational practices that safeguard the importance of human-centred activities regularly disappear in spite of our recognition of their importance, and in spite of our best intentions. Lisl Klein, who did extensive research on meaningful work, writes that the consequences of ignoring the 'soft' issues can often stay invisible until it is too late:

> It [labelling something as soft] is a way of avoiding their reality, as if human reactions are somehow ephemeral, intangible, impossible to confront. They are not. What is true is that human and social systems are very adaptable, can adjust to many situations and therefore do not appear to demand early attention as clearly as economic or technical or green factors demand it. The nature of the adjustments they make may then later be felt to be undesirable, without the causal links being recognized. (Klein 2008: 289)

The negative effects on people when their need for meaning is no longer met are well documented. Therefore many management techniques designed to speak to and draw on our deeper human needs and values have arisen over the past two decades: intrinsic motivation management, total quality management, organisational culture development, ethics management and vision and values management. More recently workplace spirituality and workplace engagement techniques have been introduced. All of these are based on the fundamental recognition that it is important to bring our humanity, our whole self, to work.

These techniques all attempt to address a conviction held by people at all levels of the organisation that there must be a better way to organise human beings. Yet, without a profound understanding of what is actually missing, it is easy to be seduced by the latest trend, bright idea or consultant panacea. This is costly to organisations financially but also breeds increasing cynicism among staff and management because fads and techniques are often superficial or piecemeal and do not address the deeper issues affecting the workplace, one of which is meaning in all its complexity. Our work points to the human need for meaning and argues that since it is already part of us we need simply to recognise it, include it and work with it to create workplaces that address both human needs and the economic imperative.

The model allows collective involvement without the suppression of the individual. It also allows us to keep all aspects of human meaning in view as we design or refine organisational structures and practices and this, as Klein says, is vitally needed.

> The biggest intellectual, methodological, and eventually cultural challenge to us is to find ways of connecting the macro and the micro, the visionary and the mundane, so that it becomes structurally impossible to consider the one without also at the same time considering the other. (Klein 2008: 71)

Complexity and fragmentation are so much part of organisational life and can so often seem so overwhelming that we can be tempted to grab a quick fix that promises respite without contemplating why such interventions needs to occur in the first place. It also means that those who object to these interventions are often at risk of being seen as 'obstructive', 'unreal' or 'change resistant' as they struggle to articulate their concerns.

The model, because it is easily grasped, helps us all to have a way of viewing what is going on in our organisation at a very profound level. This helps us to examine organisational practice and to assess what is present and what is missing so that we can, both as individuals and as an organisation, take charge in a way that really does make a difference and that is sustainable over time.

How often do we ask whether any current practice or planned change makes work more or less meaningful?

This and other questions go to the heart of creating and sustaining meaningful work. They are not simple and it can be easily understood why (and often unintentionally) the fallback position at work is to not raise such questions and treat every issue, every change, every day, as a simple set of mechanistic tasks to get through. However, if meaningful work is ignored, made invisible or is in some way seen as inferior to an ideal of the organisation as an efficient machine, issues of meaning are easily lost. When this happens there are implications for both the individual and the organisation. People cannot be treated as parts of a machine without losing connection to themselves and each other. Focusing on the question of how to manage the human being without asking who the human being is and what are their needs time and again leads to turning something as profound as the human need for meaning into an empty practice, applied when it suits an organisational goal and ignored when it is more convenient to treat human beings as a tool.

Employees often speak of their frustration that the organisation uses all the 'right language' but still not does treat them as responsible human beings. Managers too often speak of wanting to share responsibility and the need for engagement but of employees still not stepping up to the challenge. This goes to the heart of an 'us' versus 'them' impasse where it is still assumed that those lower in the organisation's hierarchy need to be motivated whereas those higher up do the motivating.

The cure to people issues at work has usually been to focus on motivational techniques. But this misses the point. Our research shows that human beings are by their very nature motivated by meaningful work, but because this is not well understood, it is often not considered and therefore unconsciously destroyed. People do not want someone else's meaning. Our research shows that they have and want their own. They do not want to be 'motivated'; they want to be given conditions that allow them to remain connected to, or enable them to reconnect with, what they consider makes their work meaningful. This is one of the key insights our work offers, because the Holistic Development Model allows you to clearly understand people's process of meaning-making and therefore to work with existing meaning—your own included. The model helps everyone recognise and factor in the human need for meaningful work and plan accordingly.

On the other hand, we see more and more good and sustainable practice in organisations that are well ahead of the pack. In other words, we live in a time in which alternatives are not only interesting ideas that may one day take place, but in which alternatives have also been shown to work, and to work sustainably. Some of these organisations no longer try to motivate people but focus on creating environments that enable people to work meaningfully in their own way (Briskin 1998); others focus on how to create environments in which people are intrinsically free and equal (Carney and Getz 2009); yet others have found that redefining their purpose has had substantial impact on the extent to which their employees experience meaningful work (Ellsworth 2002).

Chapter overview

In the previous chapters we showed how the Holistic Development Model is central to our ability to voice, be whole and take constructive responsibility between reality and inspiration. In the next three chapters we pick up each of these themes in reverse order. In Chapter 6 we start with an exploration of the tension between Inspiration and Reality in which contemporary organisations find themselves. This provides a clear context for working with the Holistic Development Model so that we can have a way to begin to prevent the complexities of organisational life from overwhelming us. Next we look at how the model helps everyone in the organisation in taking collective responsibility in relation to both Inspiration and Reality. In response to complexity, management often falls back on traditional command and control practices and structures, creating dependency. We show how the model places responsibility firmly with all members of the organisation.

In Chapter 7 we look at how to create systems that are integrated and able to respond to the needs of the whole human being and that support a unified response throughout the organisation.

In Chapter 8 we look at how the model can be used over time to encourage the ongoing voicing of meaning within organisations so that we can more often create our own solutions and do not constantly keep looking outside for the latest solution.

For each of these chapters we show how meaningful (and meaningless) work shapes, and is shaped by, organisational systems. As in the previous chapters, we draw on a combination of exercises, case studies, learning and insights from ourselves and others as well as the wisdom of scholars in organisation studies.

6

Taking responsibility between Inspiration and Reality in contemporary organisations

Any contemporary organisation needs to meet two needs. On the one hand, organisations are collectives of people, and employee well-being and productivity is enhanced when work is aligned with their humanness. Human beings need to be lifted above the drudgery of daily work and be drawn to the worthwhile purposes that their work accomplishes. On the other hand, organisations need to survive on tight budgets in the public sector or deliver attractive returns to shareholders in the private sector. This need drives the search for constant improvements in productivity, efficiency and accountability. These dual needs, which exist in both commercial and not-for-profit organisations, require energy to be constantly directed towards both inspiration and reality. At the moment, in spite of a lot of 'win–win' rhetoric, these two purposes are often addressed and experienced in isolation from each other. This has a range of negative effects.

One example is the annual inspirational speech about 'the journey we are all taking in the company', and as you walk out the door you hear employees saying, 'So, where are we going?' or 'I heard he used this exact speech up north as well', or 'What has this to do with us?' or 'Well, she obviously has never worked in our department/ branch/ area of the country'. Here we see inspiration that is not grounded. Another example is the developmental review that ideally should align personal and organisational goals but where employees come out saying, as one colleague did, 'that was the most de-motivating experience of my career'. Here we see reality that does not allow for inspiration. When executive MBA students were asked what they really thought was going on in these types of situation, which were very familiar to them as managers, one student captured the overall sentiment when he said:

> We wildly swing from inspiration to reality. We know we need to be encouraging and inspiring, we want to do this, but in response to the day-to-day reality—for example, a directive from management that staff are to focus only on profit-related goals, or that there is no money for professional development—the management badge goes on and humanity is put to the side, thus even the inspirational stuff becomes 'another thing to do' not because I don't want to be human but it is as if the manager role takes over.

In this first section we look at inspiration and the reality of organisational circumstances and how to be present to both of them at all times. We start by discussing the sources of inspiration in organisations, their natural emergence and active management.

Inspiration

As seen in Chapter 5, inspiration meets the human need for being uplifted, for new energy, hope and vision beyond the here and now. From an organisational perspective, actively managing inspiration has long been seen as a way to mobilise employees towards greater creativity and effort. In this section we first assess the nature and effectiveness of various sources of inspiration in the workplace. Next we discuss what we have learned about working with inspiration in organisations in ways that support meaningfulness.

Exercise 6.1

▶ **Purpose**

To explore inspiration in the context of your workplace.

▶ **Instructions**

Thinking over your current work, what is done that inspires you? (e.g. something said by others or shown through example, or ways of addressing a client or customer need).

Now look at what is actively designed and managed by others with the intention of inspiring you (e.g. goal setting, sales targets, inspirational speech, corporate vales).

What effect does each of these forms of inspiration have on you?

What would make the most difference in keeping your inspiration alive?

In doing Exercise 6.1 some of you will notice that it is quite small things that inspire you at work: things that you might create or be in charge of yourself or, for example, a client, student or patient thanking you for something that makes a difference to them. It might be noticing the effect your work has on another even as they continue to be occupied with their own lives; or a touching conversation with a patient, or seeing a suggestion that you have made picked up by management. And it is often from such small things that new practices are developed.

For example, in children's oncology wards in Dutch hospitals it is now common practice for nurses and parents to keep a diary together. It is a way of explaining procedure and keeping each other informed about what happened during the days and nights, but it has also become a way of making present what is sometimes unspeakable. It has a tremendous effect on the relationship between caregivers and parents and ultimately also on the quality of care. But it started with a small spark, a response to a need that was not particularly well articulated at the time, the need for a better connection between nurses and parents. One nurse started to write 'diary' notes to a parent and the parent would leave notes in return. From this came a systematic practice, but it started with just one person feeling inspired to create a better connection and then acting on her inspiration.

For many, this exercise led to conversations about making the things that inspire them more visible in their daily work:

> We are a company that creates medical equipment that makes a real difference to children who have cancer. We are of course inspired by the possibilities of improving the lives of these kids. Yet we all get caught up in the technical aspects of this work, meeting the deadlines, designing ever increasingly complex applications. Sometimes we get a letter from a parent or a kid who writes to us about the difference our equipment has made to their lives. When we talked about inspiration we decided to blow some of these letters up to poster size and put them around our workplace. We know why we are here but we forget and it is good to remind ourselves.

For others, this exercise led to conversations about how inspiration continues to be valuable even though often the organisation fails to fully realise the vision:

> Our purpose statement has in it that we 'contribute to a healthier society'. At times this has been challenging. Not all our current products are healthy. Also it is sometimes hard to find replacements that people want to buy or want to pay extra for. But it guides us in our new product development and gradually we are removing sugar etc. from a wider range of our products. I like the fact that we are reaching for the stars in spite of the practical difficulties we face.

Clearly there are many initiatives at an individual, group and organisational level that help to keep inspiration present and alive.

What we have learned from working with Inspiration at work

Simply reconnecting with our inspiration, as a deliberate and regular practice, can help us to see how to remain attuned to what is important. For example, the blown-up posters of the letters reminded the scientists and engineers why they created the medical equipment. We also need to continually assess and at times revitalise inspiration. We achieve goals and need new ones; circumstances change and may lead to inspiring opportunities. When inspiration is visible as an ongoing human need, then everyone can be responsible for keeping it alive and relevant.

Because inspiration is recognised as one of the most potent forces in mobilising people, it figures strongly in current organisational thinking and practice. Inspirational models of leadership, such as charismatic or principle-focused leadership, as well as culture, vision and values management, are ways that inspiration currently finds a place in organisational life.

What we have learned from working with inspiration, as already described in the previous chapter, is that the search for inspiration is already inherent in human beings. We were delighted to find how naturally inspiration emerged when individuals could speak to what really mattered to them and how they could sustain it. Participants would comment that this way of working with inspiration did not feel forced, but felt light and doable and energising.

Reality of Self and Circumstances in the workplace

As we saw in many of the earlier quotes and examples, reality, both of ourselves and of our circumstances, comes naturally to the fore when we talk about what inspires us. While people may experience the reality of themselves differently inside and outside the workplace, the key aspects of the theme of reality of self, that of how we confront, accept and work with the reality of our selves, tends to remain reasonably constant wherever we are. Therefore in this section we largely focus on workplace reality and how it effects inspiration, with a couple of points about reality of self in organisations later in the chapter.

Exercise 6.2

▶ **Purpose**

To explore the impact of circumstances on your inspiration.

▶ **Instructions**

At work do you (collectively) spend most of your time attaining what might be possible or battling what is at hand? Are you constantly putting out fires or have you made progress towards a common goal? Are you spending most of your time on the things that inspire you or do other things get in the way?

Is there one specific circumstance that has arisen that challenges you, or does it 'all just seem too hard'?

What ways do people at work have to support themselves in keeping going?

What do you suspect may continue to defeat them?

What participants in our workshop have noticed depends on the organisation in which they work. There is a (usually small) group that feels aligned with the overall purpose of the organisation and experiences a collective energy as a result. Often there is a group that feels aligned with the purpose of the organisation but feels that the daily battle for resources or the daily demands of the job saps their energy and they find it hard to stay in touch with why they are there in the first place. Then there is a group that feels that what the organisation is striving for is unrealistic or not shared or not lived. Finally there is a (usually small) group that is not at all aligned or no longer aligned with how the organisation defines its reason for existence, saying, for example, 'I am no longer interested in selling the latest . . . or more . . . , I just don't see how it improves people's lives', and who quite often end up saying, 'Well, I don't care about all this purpose and meaning stuff, I come to work to pay the bills.'

What we have noticed is that people do not so much struggle with the fact that a gap between inspiration and reality exists. They expect it. What drains their energy is when they feel they cannot talk about it openly and honestly. Often this results in people talking about it only in cynical 'see how we have again not done X' ways, or silently internalising their frustrations with the organisation not living up to its potential. As one of our workshop participants, who works for an electricity company, said:

> On the one hand, we had these wonderful leadership pro-grammes in which we were encouraged to live by our prin-ciples. On the other hand, if there was a price increase, no one would ask how this would affect our poorest customers.

What we have learned in working with Reality of Circumstances

Reality can be the graveyard of corporate dreams and aspirations. Reality can so easily lead to cynicism, bitterness, overwhelmingness and despair—all expressions of frustrated inspiration. Yet reality can be the source of inspiration as well. Examples where the boss and senior managers take huge pay cuts in order to keep people in jobs, or where everyone agrees to shorter hours and less pay in order to maintain their colleagues in employment, can create a sud-denly inspiring organisational culture. Many organisations for social change have been created out of an individual's response to reality such as Amnesty, Red Cross and the Samaritans. Many of the leaders that students in our management classes always hold up as exam-ples, such as Gandhi or Mandela, became leaders as a response to suffering. Reality is something we can never escape for long. Time and again we found that having Reality present in the Holistic Devel-opment Model and working with it legitimises talking about it and helps people talk about it without judgement or negativity and that this has a profound and lasting effect, as we exemplify in Case study 6.1 where Robin Burgess describes one way he uses the model.

Case study 6.1 **Reality beyond negativity**

I have worked with the Holistic Development Model as a facilitator for a number of years. In this situation I was particularly drawn to its ability as a reflective tool to deepen self-awareness while delivering a long programme of personal leadership development as part of organisational training within the police. I used the model focusing on the three axes of Being/Doing, Self/Others and Inspiration/Reality.

However, for many of them the key issue was centred on the axis of Inspiration and Reality. They struggled to accept and work with reality. They got bogged down in things not being as they should, fighting what is, rather than learning that it is not helpful, resisting the deep spiritual truth of living in the present and accepting and working with what is. That's understandable because there's a great fear that if they accept things as they are, they'll lose their vision. When they saw Inspiration and Reality out there in the PowerPoint diagram, and they graphically perceived the relation between the two—which is virtually impossible to explain verbally—they experienced a release and empowering, and began to develop some real political acumen. They realised: 'So this is what is.' And then they began to ask themselves, 'So what am I going to do and how am I going to work with it?' They experienced this as a real empowerment.

In my many years of working with people across a very broad variety of roles and organisations I have found that people often get stuck in 'drama triangles' (cf. transactional analysis). In organisations it's easy to get stuck in the drama triangle, whether in the position of 'victim' (or, in rapid switches of position, to 'persecutor' and/or 'rescuer' at times too). By focusing on the bigger areas offered by the Holistic Development Model, within the context of Reality and Inspiration, it helped them move away from that stuckness. They connected with a deeper part of themselves. People want to connect with that deeper, better part of themselves. They want to be in touch with it, and want to express it, and they don't know how to do it. They don't want to remain stuck in the drama triangle. The Holistic Development Model takes them to somewhere where they aren't stuck, to a place where they can access that non-neurotic part of themselves. It takes them deeper and they connect with areas of deep purpose, rather than the more superficial stuff.

And this view was borne out by subsequent feedback from a participant on the programme.

The Holistic Development tool was interesting to use not peruse, if you get what I mean? It wasn't until I started to articulate the words that I found my way around the model in a useful/directional way. It took me from reality to inspirational and back again many times. I found I spent a lot of time in contributing (Doing/Others quadrant). The questions, which were mainly organisational (e.g. What am I doing to bring back inspiration?), have set me thinking. On reflection I now wonder why I haven't spent more time in Development and Self-actualisation quadrants over the past 18 months, though I am aware Self is low in my priorities when there is work to be done. All in all a very useful reflective tool. It also increased the level of trust and honesty.

What we explore next is the relationship between reality and meaningfulness in organisational life. As previously said, when we do not make both of them deliberately present, they often present themselves in unhelpful and erratic ways. Because when inspiration and reality are seen totally separate from one another we notice that reality can show up in two ways: as too little reality causing loss of meaning, or as too much reality causing loss of meaning.

Too much reality

Recently one of us was in a meeting of an organisation that had decided to become more sustainable. A project group had been appointed to be in charge of the sustainability agenda. They had organised a meeting to obtain staff input.

Many people offered ideas but within a time-span of 20 minutes we heard: 'Let's be real here', said by three different people; 'Nice idea, but in the real world', from seven different people; and 'We can't even consider such an idea with the budget constraints we're facing', again said three times by different people. These responses came from the project group as well as other members in the audience.

If the audience had been a balloon one could have seen it deflate and after about 20 minutes people simply stopped offering ideas. All these phrases, which we have all heard many times, are ways of using reality as a bludgeon. It does not only kill innovation and creativity—the very things organisations say they are desperate for— but it also goes straight to the heart of our humanity. It says 'you can only be human if you grow up and see the world for what it is—my way' and 'you are not allowed to dream about future possibilities for the world'.

On another occasion, one of us observed a meeting in which a seaport company had invited the community to a meeting. The community wanted input into what was to be done with soon-to-be-vacated areas of harbour access. They were told that, in principle, the port was not against consultation but only if members of the community could 'make mature contributions that would be real'. Reality is seen to be the domain of 'grown-ups', the domain of the serious and the successful who then get to define reality for everyone else. In many cases the way reality is used is almost as a punishment for daring to dream or have an idea of anything other than business as usual.

Too much of 'the reality is . . .' or 'but in the real world . . .' becomes an excuse, a way of not engaging with or taking any action on the more challenging aspects of organisational life, or of ignoring possible new ways of doing things. It's so endemic that many people have stopped offering their new ideas. Thus we have the ironic situation where organisations spend money on programmes designed to encourage creativity and innovation and then wonder why nothing happens. A few words can stop most creativity and innovation before they are born. One group is left feeling permanently frustrated while another has a sense of being the only one who sees things 'as they really are'. In all these cases 'reality' simply prevents us from listening harder and helping to ground and birth a glimmer of an idea that might bear valuable fruit if given a bit more time and attention.

Too little reality

On the other hand we have all been in a meeting listening to some person rave on about an idea that feels quite off the planet and been tempted ourselves to want them to 'get real'. Some motivational speakers sound almost hysterical because they have become completely detached from the world as we know it. But more often in organisations we find that we are asked to go along with a type of pretence. We feel we are asked to pretend that the organisation lives by its vision statement, that people are treated as its most important asset or that the organisation is concerned about more than profit, and feel that we cannot say where this is not happening. In such situations meaning is lost precisely because it feels a mockery has been made of what we could hold dear if it were true. Douglas Ready and Jay Conger (2008), who have researched why bold visions and inspirational leadership acts fail in organisations, describe the story of a meeting of a large international finance company. The scene was carefully set; 3,500 executives had been flown in for the purpose, loud music and laser images peppered the crowd and the stage:

> The message was simple: 'We will become "the breakout firm." And to achieve breakout status we will rely on the three I's of innovation, integration, and inspiration.' Given the tight schedule of events for this one-day meeting, the CEO took no questions. But the speech had caught the executives' attention, and the new vision created a buzz of excitement.
>   Months later, the buzz had worn off. Reality had intruded, as it always does . . . In short, following their initial enthusiasm the company's senior executives were having a hard time reconciling the new vision with day-to-day realities. (Ready and Conger 2008)

This will feel very familiar to many of us. Just as we need to factor reality in to any plan in our personal lives, so we also need to do so in the workplace. Inspiration is not enough. It is as if we constantly seize the one and lose sight of its connection with the other. But as we focus on one to the exclusion of the other, as we have seen in the examples above, we run the risk of becoming unable to access creativity (too much reality) or unable to ground inspiration and make it work (too little reality). The first leads to resignation and the second to cynicism, both of which infest our organisations.

The trick is to work with both in view, and that is what the model helps us to do.

Working with Inspiration and Reality in organisations

Inspiration and Reality can so easily appear as opposing forces. The model immediately makes it clear how they are intertwined, how one creates the opening for the other, how they are both, in some way, sides of the same thing.

Our work with the model has helped us reframe our own understanding of inspiration and reality. Viewed in relation to inspiration, reality helps us to get in touch with the more positive attributes of constraint, practicality and the earth itself. As one workshop participant said, 'The value of reality is that when it hits us, it is often the only time that we notice what's happening. It forces us to pay attention to what's happening.' When paying attention in this sense, reality so often becomes the well-spring of innovation and creativity. Parker Palmer in *The Active Life* (1990: 24, 25) suggests that,

> Truth is always preferable to illusion, no matter how closely the illusion conforms to our notion of the good—or how far the truth diverges from it . . . [This is because] when we reflect on the nature of action, we inevitably come to the question 'What is real?' Every action originates in some assessment of reality, no matter how mistaken. No action will have lasting effects if it is inconsistent with reality. Ultimately, action will help to reveal what the reality is, if we pay attention to its outcomes.

Seeing what is real in this sense helps us to hone our work, refine our ideas, rethink our analysis, open ourselves up to increased creativity and finally experience the joy of making things happen 'in the real world'. And for all the many dreamers and creatives among us, there is a deep satisfaction in grounding ideas and seeing them bear fruit in reality.

At an organisational level, working constructively with reality can again provide inspiration. One of us remembers seeing on the walls of an advertising agency founder David Ogilvy's mantra, 'Grant me the freedom of a tight brief', a statement that sums up some of the positive aspects of reality in work, arguing that it is limits and restrictions that force the mind to think in new ways.

On an individual level, the area of Reality of Self in organisations, confronting inauthenticity enables people in organisations to grow into human beings who can find meaning for their life even when fully aware of their limitations. Schwartz (1995: 242) writes that

> the capacity to accept human reality for what it is, in
> oneself as well as others, makes for the possibility of an
> identification with others that is more real and therefore
> more profound than that of mutual idealization in the ego
> ideal.

Grounding inspiration in both the reality of our selves and our circumstances in organisations can, most importantly, ensure that everyone is, and remains, engaged in a vision. In this sense we can argue that reality can be both a testing ground and a source of ongoing inspiration.

Working with the model helps open up opportunities for everyone to take charge of meaning. It does not have to be left to the CEO: 'Our boss came to us and said: "I need help; I'm not sure what to do next." There was an odd relief in that, even if we did not have the immediate answer.'

Vision and possibility can be maintained in spite of our flaws when these are directly recognised:

> We had a lot of conflict; we would talk about empowering
> each other but personalities would get in the way. But we
> were all so passionate about our work and could accept
> each other's flaws and discuss our individual and collective
> shortcomings.

The model helps us see how meaning is created in the constructive way in which we work with inspiration grounded within the reality of ourselves and our circumstances, so that with both in view we can use one to enrich the other. It simply allows an organisation, its employees and its decision-makers, to keep present at all times that organisational life by definition takes place in a field of complexity and tension, but keeping this visible through working with the model we can find ways to integrate them. The model has a way of presenting inspiration and reality that enables us to address both constructively and that makes sure that people do not become stuck in too much or too little reality or inspiration. It takes them to a place where they can access that larger, deeper part of themselves. It takes them deeper and they connect with areas of profound purpose, rather than anything more superficial.

In this section we saw that this is not only the case for those who work with the model on their own organisational issues, but also for those who facilitate such work (be they a fellow team member, consultant or leader) as they have this at their fingertips at all times. Thus it enables them at any time to focus group processes on what is really profound and foundational, rather than get stuck in detail, negativity or inappropriate 'rescuing'.

Taking collective responsibility between Inspiration and Reality

Once we can work with both Inspiration and Reality inextricably linked and in view at the same time, we can, as we saw in Chapter 5, more easily take responsibility both individually and collectively. In fact between Inspiration and Reality is the place where we build muscle. In Chapter 5 we saw that taking responsibility is absolutely essential to living meaningfully. However, organisations present an interesting challenge to this. On the one hand, organisations want responsible individuals who are proactive, accountable and mature. On the other hand, organisations often put processes in place that convey a subtext of 'we want you to be responsible, but we are not so sure that you can be, hence we need to put lots of management and control into place'. Unfortunately employees often respond to this subtext with immaturity and co-dependency to which the organisational response is to put more management and control in place, resulting in a vicious cycle. It is in this complex context that we examine how the model can help all members of the organisation to take responsibility collectively.

Exercise 6.3

▶ **Purpose**

To participate in setting meaningful objectives and to evaluate these in meaningful ways.

▶ **Instructions**

Go back to one of the most recent values exercises your organisation did. This could be writing a strategic plan, setting mission, vision or values statements or participating in a training programmes on teamwork or integrity.

Evaluate the extent to which everyone:

1. Participated in arriving at these values, ideals or purposes
2. Is currently participating in upholding them

Chances are your organisation has a written set of values. A growing number of organisations do and it is estimated that around 80% of all companies and not-for-profit organisations now have such statements. These values can describe attitudes or ways of doing things, as well as ideal outcomes such as 'teamwork', 'the customer is always right', 'employees are valued above all else' or 'integrity'. In many cases such values are prescribed by management, and employees are given training to 'develop their understanding' of these values. In other cases a more bottom-up approach is taken, in which employees are asked what they consider to be the most important values that the organisation already has or should strive for. These are then collated and, usually with the aid of communication experts, written down in a way that combines all input but that, unfortunately, is often no longer recognised by employees as their own. A human resources manager in a company that tries to be values-driven, reported after doing this exercise:

> The CEO asked me to collate what employees valued in this company and also what they felt should be the overall values and purpose statement of this company. We went through some extensive consultation with various groups

of employees, ensuring they all had some input. A few days later the CEO emailed 'can you just get some of those phrases to me and I'll pick the most relevant, positive and telling examples and arrive at a statement'.

We came across only a very small number of research participants who had examples where the whole process was co-owned.

What we have learned

Value-identification practices hold great promise and considerable resources are often invested in them. Both employees and managers have opportunities to articulate what is important to them as human beings, and there is evidence that these statements can increase accountability, clarify expectations and increase employee pride and commitment.

At the same time, in doing this particular exercise we noticed that although most companies understand that it is important that everyone in the organisation owns the end result, it seems incredibly difficult to facilitate and sustain processes that ensure collective input and collective responsibility for monitoring. Workshop participants reported several effects:

- When they are not co-created there is no buy-in, while at the same time co-creation can be an unwieldy process and is often hard to facilitate

- While much time is often spent on drafting and redrafting values statements, far less time is usually spent on ensuring that values and behaviour are aligned or designing ways for this to happen. When it is, this is usually done in a controlling rather than participative way. As one of the workshop participants said, 'First they ask us what is meaningful to us. Next they tell us how we should live by it. They never asked our ideas about that part.'

- Values statements can be treated with cynicism or even contempt if they are seen to be another way of getting more out of employees

In the next section we look at a case study in which the Holistic Development Model is used to collectively arrive at and implement a mission statement. We summarise how the model helps all members of the organisation to take responsibility and conclude with a comment from organisation studies scholars about the topic.

Connecting organisational vision and personal responsibility

One of our colleagues who regularly works with the Holistic Development Model is Patricia Greenhough. In Case study 6.2 she describes how she has used the model to arrive at a vision statement for a community organisation. The case study spans four years.

Case study 6.2 **A bottom-up vision statement connecting each individual**

I always use the model in several stages. First I focus on connecting the individual to what is meaningful to them personally. Next I focus on the individual's role in the organisation. Then I focus on the organisation itself. I have found this process makes a big difference if you ask the individual to reflect on what is meaningful for them before you start to focus on the organisation because:

- I am passionate about the well-being of individuals
- The organisation can only be whole to the extent that the individuals within it are whole
- When you start with the organisation, the individual still has the question of 'what about me' going on, and rightly so, so you might as well get that on the table first. When people have been able to attend to what is meaningful to them they bring peace to the process
- If the individual feels nourished throughout the process they find a richness and quality in their contributions. They operate from a higher place
- In subsequent sessions I have seen that this really helps people to connect the personal to the organisational and back again. It makes it so easy to generate the practical expression of such

things as a vision and mission statement because people are already so connected to it

In the next stage, we focused on the organisational vision. In this case the members of the board and paid staff were involved. For the process, we used brainstorming. People came up with words that were important to them, made sentences, used dictionaries, etc. It was a vibrant process and we kept paring back from a huge amount of words. People kept focusing on how they were going as a group while also checking in with how they were doing themselves. All the words and sentences were eventually pared back to a single statement that said, 'a vibrant place of hope and connection, standing tall, reaching all'.

One of the things that also became apparent was that the paid workers had a vision they had not shared with the board. For this reason it was so important to have everyone, regardless of their position, involved in this process. As one of the board directors wrote: 'This day captured the needs of the organisation, helped us to focus and prioritise and re-energised and renewed the vision and purpose of our existence . . . thank you, we all took away something special for ourselves as well as some great thinking for the organisation. We have our vision statement proudly displayed and have already used it in one of our funding applications.'

I worked with the community group over the next few years and am still doing so with an annual strategic planning and review day. We use the model less overtly as it has become integrated into what they do. It was used to decide whom they wanted to attract as new board members and to more clearly define the role of volunteers, coming up with a job description for the volunteers using the qualities from the model.

Some outcomes:

- The vision statement was already used the next day in a funding application
- The city council adopted the some of the board's vision in their own 2025 community development plan
- The community organisation has gone from strength to strength

As one of the staff members wrote: 'I feel we have developed wonderful, safe, practical systems that simply nourish and wow my work and workplace. Thank you, it never feels like training.'

We have found the model to be very useful in empowering people in several ways:

- It starts from an emancipatory world-view. It is based on our findings that everyone actually knows what is meaningful and meaningless, what they wish and do not wish to contribute their life force to. Time and time again we have seen how the depth and calibre of people simply rises to the top when they are engaged in questions of meaning. This happens whether or not it is the first time that they have been asked to speak about such things. Each time the model reveals that 'people already know what is meaningful to them'. When we work with the model, although we know this is what happens and have it reinforced by case studies as above, we are constantly moved by the depth, richness and wisdom of ordinary people when they are given a simple and safe way to reveal this

- We have found that the model, and particularly the two-step process as described in Case Study 6.2, profoundly connects personal and organisational purpose. The model is very effective in connecting the individual sense of meaning to the bigger picture and creating a collective sense of meaningfulness which endures

- We find again and again that from that profound place of meaning, people are ready to work maturely and constructively

- The model helps peel things back to what is simple and doable. This leads to values statements that are real and have everyone's buy-in. And as we could see from the case study, people immediately take steps to put the vision in action

- Finally, and very importantly, the Holistic Development Model can remain a constant reminder, one that legitimises asking questions about meaning. For those who work with it a lot, such as the community group in Case study 6.2, it becomes a lens through which everything can be planned and evaluated

What others have thought

Management research and practice has been based on the assumption that leadership and organisational culture can and should provide employees with meaning. While some authors (and managers) focus on the need to draw on the resources of everyone in the organisation, often the employee is treated as an empty vessel, a recipient of meaning rather than a co-constructor of meaning. Such research and practice also assumes that factors that contribute to meaningful work, such as a sense of belonging that a 'strong' organisational culture might encourage, can be understood in isolation from factors that contribute to meaningless work, such as excessive control.

As the interest of the scholarly and business communities in 'the management of meaning' developed, increasingly questions have been raised about whether healthy outcomes for individuals and society are achieved when meaning becomes a form of normative control—that is, as a way to keep people in line (Ashforth and Vaidyanath 2002; Casey 1999; Willmott 1993). In addition, organisations have increasingly found that such forms of control are in fact ineffective and unsustainable; they just do not achieve the desired levels of buy-in. It is therefore increasingly found that 'the management of meaning' may in fact reduce the experience of meaningful work. Meaninglessness arises when meaning is either substituted or controlled, because in both these cases it is no longer authentic for the individual or the group. Sievers (1994: 26-27) writes:

> As meaning gets lost (and with it the ability or quality of meaning as a coordinating and integrating source for one's own actions as well as for the interactions with others) motivation has to be invented. Through motivation the lack of meaning of work becomes substituted or converted into the question 'how does one get people to act and produce under conditions in which they normally would not be "motivated" to work?'

The question that scholars and practitioners then started asking was, 'how do we empower people?' Thus a lot of discussion about empowerment followed. However, this has led to what is referred to as bogus empowerment (Ciulla 2004). For example, Parry and

Bryman (2006: 447), in summarising leadership research from the mid-1980s until the present, notice that leadership is still 'seen as a process whereby the leader identifies for subordinates a sense of what is important—defining organizational reality for others' and where 'the leader gives a sense of direction and of purpose through the articulation of a compelling world-view'.

If this vision is not provided by the leader, it is usually done so by a consultant. The ongoing preoccupation with culture change has 'meant the elaboration of new programmes embodied in mission statements, visions and new value systems facilitated by a plethora of consultancy interventions, aimed at reinventing both the identity of the corporation and of the subjects within it' (Costea *et al.* 2008: 661).

However, recently cracks are appearing in this approach of top-down management of meaning and many organisations are looking for alternatives, as they realise they have to find better ways to connect personal and organisational meaning.

First, it is increasingly recognised that the purpose of the company itself needs to rise above the immediate reality of the organisation. Companies are therefore increasingly defining 'purpose beyond profit'. The reason for this is simple: it meets the human need for inspiration and drives sustainable success and long-term profit:

> Each company has the core purpose of providing goods or services that meet customer needs or aspirations and yield a profit. In great companies, purpose extends beyond short-term profit and the creation of shareholder value. It often encompasses a longer-term vision to make a contribution to improve people's lives and be a force for progress in the world. Together with principles and values, purpose is what a great company stands for and would stand by even if adhering to them resulted in a competitive disadvantage, missed opportunity, or increased costs. (Jackson and Nelson 2004: 299)

Second, it is increasingly recognised that everyone needs to share such a purpose for the organisation to be able to deliver on it. Otherwise it will simply not only fail, but also not connect to meaningful work for all members of the organisation. CEOs therefore have really recognised that they need to 'get everyone in the organisation on board'. For example, Jeff Hollender, co-founder of Seventh Generation Inc, describes a situation (Hollender and Breen 2010) where he wanted to be transparent about the fact that one of their products, due to the lack of a suitable supplier, did not quite meet its own standards with regard to non-toxic brands. The leadership team wondered why anyone should know this and were concerned that the competitors would have a field-day with it. Hollender realised that as deeply committed as he was to transparency as a moral principle, he had forgotten to bring everyone else along in this: 'I hadn't brought anyone along with me by facilitating discussions, providing education and context about what we were about to do.' On reflection, he writes, 'What most clearly emerged from this often excruciating process was that the discussions and debates regarding what constituted a meaningful and beneficial level of disclosure were in and of themselves worthwhile, and were indeed drivers of change.'

Finally, it has become increasingly well documented that the members of an organisation need to take collective responsibility for purpose beyond profit. For organisations to outperform others, they need to have the courage to challenge long-held management beliefs about human nature and employees and radically depart from the traditional command-and-control structures, rules and policies. People who are not treated as equals will leave you alone with your vision. The organisation must let people self-direct and grow (Carney and Getz 2009).

Summary

Working with the model addresses all of these insights into management and organisation. After working with the model people usually put the best of themselves forward and more consistently search for the greater good that the company can achieve. Working with the model very effectively connects personal and organisational purpose, vision, principles and values. Everyone in the organisation can be on board from the outset. Finally, working with the model is liberating for management because people more readily ask to take increased responsibility and share responsibility for keeping the vision alive.

In the next chapter we will address how the model aids in integrating the often fragmented messages and practices in organisations that can strip meaning from people's working lives.

7

Creating practices and systems that have integrity and respond to the whole human being

Organisations are often experienced as a series of disconnected, competing and conflicting activities, practices and rules. This causes those within them to fragment their focus and feel as if they are never achieving enough. The Holistic Development Model helps identify activities as either supporting or detracting from meaningful work. People can then begin to find ways of connecting and integrating organisational practices and so increase a sense of wholeness and shared purpose. As one practitioner who works with the model said, 'You can't achieve the mission, the organisational purpose, if you're not whole.' Rather than start with an exercise, this time we start with a case study, 7.1. In it the consultant reveals the problems that arise from a fragmented or limited focus and how working with the model addresses this. After that we introduce an exercise that allows you, your team and your organisation to understand where energy goes at work and how to quickly adjust this if it becomes unbalanced, picking up the axes of Being and Doing, and Self and Others. Next we present a case study, 7.2, on one organisational practice, the performance review, and describe how the model can create a more holistic experience out of what is often a part of fragmented organisational practices. To put our experiences in context, we conclude with what others have written about the effects of wholeness and fragmentation on organisations.

But first we begin with some examples of how Dave Burton has used the model over many years.

Case study 7.1 **On time management**

I am a professional development coach, working with people at all levels within large organisations. Their roles include team leaders, line managers, senior managers, general managers and CEOs and I use the term 'responsibility holders' as an overall description of them.

My rationale for using the model in this context is that it addresses a need that I regularly come across: the need for people to be able to see their work as more than just a process of 'delivering the goods' or 'meeting the targets' (both are terms I use for Service to Others on the model). I have reached this conclusion because I noticed that people who are heavily focused on production, delivery, processing, etc. can become distant, depressed and disillusioned with their work. They sense a lack of purpose despite being very busy and get to a point where they see getting busier as the solution to their problem. From my observations as a coach, getting busier is the last thing they need, because their life has already become imbalanced to the extent, in some cases, of showing early stages of 'workaholism'.

This situation is exacerbated in many organisations because key performance indicators have been, and often still are, very focused on the achievement of goals, most of which are around production and processing. Achievement of these goals often excludes activity in the other three quadrants of the model: development of either self or team, building and maintaining relationships, and representing themselves or expressing their full potential.

My first exposure to the model highlighted exactly this situation in my own consulting business. During the mid-1990s, while being very busy 'delivering the goods' in New Zealand, I was carrying out a professional development project for managers in a major petrochemical plant in Saudi Arabia. I was about to travel there for the fourth time and had a sense that they were expecting something new and fresh

from me. The managers liked the work that I was doing but were looking for more, and I had a sense that I didn't have anything new to take
to them. One could say that coincidentally, about that time, I attended
one of the early workshops on the Holistic Development Model. I
arrived at the workshop feeling somewhat glum and desperate but
quickly started to engage with the model and started to see how I
could apply it in the business/corporate context.

As people in the group started to work with the model on their own
issues and questions, I noticed a change of atmosphere in the room. I
also noticed how quickly I became still and attentive. It wasn't intellec-
tually based. It was based on my experience of being in the Developing the Inner Self quadrant of the model. I simply found myself feeling
better, looking forward to the upcoming project and having a strong
sense of being newly resourced as I considered the other three quadrants as new ways of naming and thinking about my role.

A few weeks later I travelled to Saudi Arabia with this model and
used it consistently in my professional development and coaching
sessions with managers during my visit. Their response to it was iden-
tical to mine.

A specific example was one manager who was suffering quite significant stress, so I worked through the model with him. We talked
about the scope and the potential benefits of spreading his time
between each of the quadrants. It became clear that he had not done
any self-development work for some time. He had been put into a
new and quite senior management role with very little support or training. He was by nature a very relationship-oriented person but found
he had absolutely no time to spend with his people other than in a
task-related mode. Because he ended up feeling stressed, his ability
to represent himself and what he was doing—my term for Expressing
Full Potential—limited his confidence. He found himself totally focused
on 'delivering the goods' (Service to Others) and meeting the expectations and demands that landed on his desk from all around him: in a
400-acre petrochemical plant there are a lot of those demands!

As a result of working through the model and assessing that he was
spending about 95% of his time in the 'delivering the goods' quadrant, he then formulated plans to adjust his workload and delegate
a significant part of the operational work that he had been doing. He
enlisted the help of his PA to screen work that was coming to him, to
ensure that a more organised and sorted pile arrived on his desk. He
was then able to refocus on other things that made his work meaningful such as building relationships and representing himself more ably.
Within a few weeks his stress levels had reduced considerably and he

went on first to enjoy his job and consequently to prove very successful at it.

My response to the model was very positive as well. Not only had I found the model personally useful and encouraging, I had seen it work well on the other side of the world in a different culture from my own. Its effectiveness across that range of diversity indicated to me that it was a model with depth and appeal to humanity as a whole.

I have continued to use the model with good effect when working with time management issues in my work in New Zealand. An example involves a man in his early 30s who was managing the IT help desk for a large organisation. By definition this job was a highly delivery-based Service to Others as it was almost solely based on receiving and responding to customer calls. The manager was effectively running a call centre, and, again almost by definition, carrying out a task that could never be completed. He had become totally focused on 'delivering the goods' and it quickly became apparent that he was suffering from minor depression. His work was suffering, his relationships with family and colleagues were suffering, he was getting more and more frustrated and as a result he was actually doing his job less and less well.

I just drew a cross on a piece of paper, named each of the four quadrants of the model, then asked him to indicate approximate percentages of how he was spending his time. The division was 90–95% of the time in 'delivering the goods' with the remaining 5–10% being split between the other three quadrants. It very quickly made visible that he was using his time in an seriously unbalanced way and was also missing out on the range of activities necessary to sustain a healthy life.

We began by building an action plan to help him address what turned out to be one of the more strategic aspects of his role, namely how to develop good relationships with his clients other than by just providing them with a response at the moment when they had a problem. So he embarked on a programme of going out to meet his clients in the areas that reported the most problems. He met them individually and in groups and (combining building relationships and representing oneself) introducing himself and his team to them. This meant that the callers weren't just dealing with faceless scapegoats on whom they could take out their frustrations. By doing this, he was also addressing the first quadrant, by personally growing to do the job that was actually being asked of him.

There were three consequences to his actions. First, his health, attitude and sense of purpose improved immediately; he regained a sense of being in charge of himself. Second, the number of calls coming into the centre dropped, and third, the nature of these calls changed from being hostile, aggressive and unfriendly to being cheerful and friendly. The calls became a 'request for help' rather than a 'blaming for the problem'. Obviously this made a huge difference to everyone concerned.

What we have learned

Case study 7.1 quickly reveals why working with the model is so effective in overcoming imbalance and fragmentation:

- Working with the model works on the self as well as the other. It is therefore not a technique that is imposed on others, but rather a journey that is taken together. This means that working with the model does not become just another thing to do, in itself causing more imbalance, but allows for processes that are, in themselves, whole and integrating

- The model allows people to see particular actions in relation to the whole. As a result they immediately see where they spend too much of their time, as well as what they lose out on, and the consequences of this

- The model does not distinguish between different life roles. Thus, while it might be very useful to focus on one life role such as work, people can also quickly discern how unbalanced work behaviour causes unbalanced family behaviour

- When the model is used to diagnose the problem, the solutions to the problem are also holistic. The model does not prescribe specific solutions for each pathway. Rather it becomes an internalised perspective from which people can see the whole and then respond more from the whole of themselves. This helps them put solutions into place that meet the whole of self and are likely to be long-lasting

- Working on the under-represented quadrants has the effect of making the work in the over-represented quadrant more effective

Being and Doing, Self and Others in our workplaces and organisations

In Case study 7.1, specific quadrants of the model were used to check for wholeness and balance. In Chapter 4, we also looked at how the model quickly allows you to scan for Being and Doing, Self and Others and how this is another helpful way to discern patterns that cause fragmentation or create wholeness. In this section we look at the relationship between Being and Doing in your work, and in the next we will look at Self and Others at work.

Being and Doing

How much time do you get to *be* at work compared with the pressure to *do*?

Exercise 7.1

► **Purpose**

To notice where most of your energy goes at work.

► **Instructions**

Think about your most recent week(s) at work. Where did the 'need to get on with it' distract from the need to dwell on an issue, reflect and take a bit more time to make a decision? Where did time/economic pressure take away from human interaction or hearing the concerns of others in meetings, etc.?

Notice how this has affected you and those you work with.

We find that because the Holistic Development Model distinguishes Being from Doing in the workplace it becomes possible to evaluate organisational life in terms of the time and the skills that Being requires. This enables fruitful reflections about the extent to which we allow ourselves to be in organisations, the consequences of this and a chance to create a range of possible corrective actions.

We find that the language that participants use for the Being and Doing distinction at organisational level is quite diverse. They may distinguish 'being' and 'doing' or 'action and reflection/contemplation' or 'running around' versus 'stillness' or the 'mindful' organisation versus the 'mindless' organisation.

A common theme in these conversations is that time is a scarce commodity in organisational life. Organisations are experiencing a permanent whitewater of change, the pressures of intensified demands for efficiency, accountability and transparency, and a relentless pursuit of future outcomes, all resulting in most employees feeling under constant pressure.

Occasionally the concept of the inert organisation arises, where there might be too much Being (for example, a family-run organisation that does not change because it wants to keep the comfortable feelings of belonging) but by and large the main problem is the loss of time to 'be' in organisations and the effect this has on experiencing work as meaningful.

Pressure goes to the heart of several issues that have the potential to diminish meaningfulness in work. Some of the themes that we often hear about in such conversations are that:

- People are not able to keep hold of what is good and what they value in periods of rapid change

- Bad decisions are made towards the end of meetings when under time pressure someone says 'OK, let's just get on with it'

- People lose touch with themselves when they have no time to reflect and find themselves in roles or positions that they don't like, asking themselves 'How did I end up doing this work within the organisation? I'm really much more interested in . . . or better at . . .'

- People feel lonely or isolated in the organisation because they no longer have time to have a break together or form meaningful relationships with customers

- The most important conversations are always put on the back burner because the more immediate and urgent always takes precedence, giving people a sense of futility because they can no longer retain any connection to the larger and deeper aspects of meaningful living and work

The model creates a legitimate space from where to ask questions about the need to simply 'be' in an organisation and to notice what we gain and lose as a result of both Being and Doing. It helps us do this in the workplace as both individuals or in teams.

However, in many organisations the focus on Doing is so excessive that the model can be used to simply raise awareness of the distinct nature of Being. We can see an example of this in Case study 7.2, where Robin Burgess again shows the use of the tension aspects of the model.

Case study 7.2: **On deeper reflection**

I have used the model a lot and adapt it for particular situations where I feel it is most needed. I find, for example, that it is particularly useful in helping people who are primarily left-brain dominant (or what in Myers-Briggs Type Indicator [MBTI] preferences would be high on sensing and/or thinking). They find the Holistic Development Model offers a simple and effective way to reflect especially where self-reflection is an important skill to have or develop.

I have found that members of the police tend to be high on the sensing and thinking preference in the MBTI. They like to work with and think about the concrete. If you ask them to reflect they don't easily know what to do. So if you say to them, 'Think about the journey of your career', they would not necessarily feel comfortable and it might not be very productive. Using the model with a specific focus as I did leverages awareness and an experience of deeper reflection because the three axes—Self/Other, Being/Doing, Inspiration/Reality—have an accessibility as a prompt that I've not seen in any other model.

What also became clear was that the axes were specifically valuable, in this case particularly the tension between Being and Doing, because Being foxes some people in that left-brain environment. They haven't got any reference points for Being. So just introducing it through the Holistic Development Model stimulated another level of potential awareness that they connected with a bit more.

The value of this approach is echoed by a consultant in leadership in Case study 7.3.

Case study 7.3 **On leadership**

It is so important to have a way to show people that Being is important in leadership. If they focus just on more Doing they so often fail to be effective as leaders. But I've found it hard to explain, especially to the sort of people who are often in leadership positions because they are already pretty accomplished at Doing. I found that if I put the model up on the board and gave some examples—comparing the Being of Mandela with the Being of Hitler, for example—we could distinguish something of real value. After all, in terms of 'activity', Hitler is more successful; in terms of Being, Mandela is of another calibre altogether. I'd then ask them to compare other leaders that we all knew. Then Being started to appear in their reflective journals, and they began to enquire into their own Being. I don't know any other way of making the distinction and its importance so clear.

What others have written about our ability to 'be' in organisations

The rhythm of organisational life remained largely unchanged over most of the 20th century. Work and home were for many still clearly separated, the demand to be available 24/7 had not yet arrived, and many businesses, public service and community organisations were reasonably well funded. The 21st century has come to signify tremendous speed and pressure. As Peter Senge wrote in *Presence*:

> It's almost as if we're living in a split world. On the one hand, many people are experiencing a profound opening. But we're also experiencing a build-up of pressure, tension and anxiety. Time is speeding up. The people and organizations we work with are just like me, struggling to simultaneously speed up and slow down. As the need for reflection and deeper learning grows, the pressures against that need being fulfilled grow too. (Senge *et al*. 2004: 221)

A wide range of current trends have been identified that lead to ever-increasing pressures in organisations. Examples are increasing global competition, the 24/7 demand, under-funding in the public and voluntary sector and techno-stress. Meaningfulness is lost because individuals can no longer take the time to simply be (companionable, compassionate) with clients, colleagues or patients and experience a constant feeling of stress as a result of multi-tasking, being constantly on call, information overload, etc.

Vaill, in *Learning as a Way of Being*, discusses the value of Being in relation to learning in an organisational context. He suggests that individuals in organisations need to engage in a learning process that is 'more personal, more present, and more continual than institutional learning' (Vaill 1996: 55), 'a way of framing or interpreting all experience as a learning opportunity or learning process' (51), in which learning 'is not a list of tips or techniques but a whole posture towards our experience' (100), a posture that requires awareness of, and response to, one's own and the other's being.

This points to the benefits for both individuals, and ideally organisations, of a more unified way of being. Beyond the immediacy of organisational life there has also been a substantial amount written on the effects of the accelerating pace of society as a whole. For example, John Dewey (2010) writes about the weakening of civic behaviour because people simply have no time to engage in their communities. He writes that the ties that hold people together are numerous but often subtle, invisible and intangible and that it takes time to translate those bonds into positive action. Similarly Scheuerman (2010) talks about the fact that most of us feel far too busy to devote attention to basic activities of democratic citizenship—such as becoming informed about issues. We have become disconnected from each other and from these vital aspects of life. Hence work causes us to lose meaning as it takes our time and energy away from other, bigger concerns facing us as members of our local communities and as global citizens.

Robinson *et al.* (1999) point out that the fact that many of us feel rushed and tired by the day's end is not merely the result of inefficient personal time budgeting. Yes, it is true that many individuals may spend too much time watching TV, but at the same time extreme work demands are endemic to modern society and our resulting behaviour is not simply a product of irrational and morally deplorable personal choices—if watching television is morally deplorable—but also a result of genuine fatigue.

In addition, the ability to be and engage in collective organisational reflection is increasingly related to good ethical practice. Goodpaster points out that organisations that really want to be ethically discerning require humility. This requires having the time for collective reflection and treating each other as equals given that anyone within and outside the organisation is capable of identifying promising new directions for the organisation. Goodpaster understands reflectiveness as a 'cultural disposition' that can 'encourage periodic relief from goal-directedness and busy-ness of everyday worklife' (2000: 196). Reflection benefits from an open attitude and is not assisted by impatience for immediate results. 'Organizations, like persons, can suffer from the pathology of activism, the misplaced devotion of never stopping to reflect on their missions. An organizational culture can be too busy or too focussed to think—to be aware of what it is doing' (2000: 197).

In this section we have touched on the profound tension between Being and Doing and commented on how we need to find a way to do both, although they often seem to be in opposition. In the next section we explore the other fundamental tension the model identifies, between Self and Others.

Self and Others in our workplaces and organisations

How does this tension find expression at work?

Exercise 7.2

▶ **Purpose**

To reflect on the extent to which the practices (culture, management focus, etc.) in your organisation encourage self-interested behaviour versus other interested behaviour.

▶ **Instructions**

Working with or without the model, on your own or in a group, reflect on the extent to which the practices in your organisation encourage self-interested behaviour (individual professional development opportunities, career advancement, individualised

➔

performance bonuses) versus other interested behaviour (team bonuses, opportunities for everyone to consider taking a pay cut or working shorter hours rather than numerous redundancies).

Now reflect on the extent to which the organisation focuses on its own interests compared with those of other stakeholders such as the customer or the local community.

What is the effect of what you notice here on you, your colleagues and the organisation as a whole?

In discussing this tension with people inside and outside organisations we were again struck by how helpful it was for people first to map the extent to which they were able to look after both their own needs and the needs or demands of others in their organisation and, second, to understand the extent to which organisational practices caused these patterns. What was also interesting was that many felt they were too self-oriented when they did look after themselves ('If no one looks after me I need to put some boundaries in place for myself and say no to excessive overtime, but I always find it so hard to do') while at the same time they told us stories of incredible generosity in helping others by mentoring, doing extra work to lighten the load for others and standing up for the rights of others. Again, most people felt they did not have the balance quite right but all commented on how helpful it was to make the range of tensions to do with Self and Others visible to themselves, and to each other. Some themes arose regularly:

- **Protecting the Self versus addressing common concerns.** When do we speak up in organisations? When is it risky to speak up? When does it feel selfish or irresponsible not to speak up? How much time do we spend on 'causes' compared with attending to the work that we need to do, or the work that enhances our career progress? When do we follow our own guidance, and when do we follow the rules of organisations especially if these conflict with our own values? For example, in a local organisation, although employees are really committed to sustainability, as is the organisation, it has been hard to keep the sustainability interest group going because work demands are continually increasing

- **Controlling versus letting Others be.** When do we feel the need to do it ourselves, to be in control, to be in charge? When do we let others take charge or lead the way? When do we trust others to do the work well? Obviously this can relate to delegation, but it can also relate to things such as organisational strategy where in some organisations everyone is invited to contribute and in others it is left to only a few

- **Protecting the Self from overwork versus the needs of client/patients/customers.** When do we go the extra mile? When do we start to feel exhausted or abused? For example, as workplaces become more continually pressured we notice more examples of employees refusing to do extra work, or insisting on taking their holidays rather than work through them

A rather different use of Self and Others in terms of work is covered in Case study 7.4.

Case study 7.4 Balancing the way people perceive a profession

I work in the arts sector and a constant concern is the appallingly low wages that so many people work for in this industry. In my workshops on professional development or how to make some sort of living as an artist, I have been constantly struck by the way the arts are seen in society. Mostly artists are seen as 'making a lifestyle choice' or 'being self-indulgent', because art so often focuses on self expression. Therefore they are often asked, 'When are you going to get a real job?' For example, you say 'I'm a doctor' and everyone knows that you save lives. They can understand why you're valuable. You say 'I'm an artist' and the conversation just dies, or you find yourself being introduced as 'the arty-farty one', which shows in how little esteem the arts are held. When I talk to artists their main reason for their choice of career is their 'passion' (which could be seen as vocation rather than lifestyle choice) but there is virtually no conversation about what the arts contribute to society and so society seldom sees the value of the arts.

So over the past years I have been using the Self and Others axis from the model as a way to highlight this. I start by asking them why they are artists. I usually get replies that are mostly about 'passion' or some version of it. I write this up on the whiteboard. Then I put the model on the board. We then look at the list they've given me and I ask, 'So where do your answers lie on the model?' They can see that they all sit in the Self category, with a bit of Unity with Others in that they are part of a group of passionate people. 'What is missing do you think?' It's pretty obvious that it's Service to Others, so I lead into a conversation about what the arts contribute: things like vision, reflecting back alterative views about society, making visible what can be otherwise not noticed, capturing the spirit of a country, an idea, a possibility, etc. We then link this into the approach they take to their design of their CV, business card and portfolio.

What has emerged from all this is a radically different conversation on the contribution the arts make to society and a stronger sense of the value they offer and an ability to speak confidently about this. If I had not known about the model I don't think I could have worked out that this was the problem facing the industry. Now it is so clear to me. Being able to explain their profession in terms of the contribution the arts make to society has helped many of these young artists value their skills and talents and negotiate their careers and salaries more positively.

While this case study looks more at the position of an industry, it highlights the value of the Holistic Development Model in enabling people to see how the fundamental tensions in human meaning, which are so often invisible or unexpressed, can shape the way a profession is seen and valued. As with Case study 7.3 in Being and Doing, so often, once the distinction is clearly made, participants can be in control in an area where before they had no analysis that empowered them.

In the next section of this chapter we look at how the nature of tensions are discussed in the management literature.

What others have written on tensions in organisations

There is an increasing range of literature on the concepts of paradox and tension in organisations. Senge (1997) introduced the concept of addressing tension as part of organisational learning; Drucker

(1994) and Handy (1994) both discuss the concept that successful organisations of the future will be able to reconcile a series of seemingly irreconcilable paradoxes; and McKenzie (1996) sees paradox as the next strategic dimension. This type of conceptual literature proposes that contradictions do not necessarily show a theory or practice to be at fault, but rather that there may be an unavoidable tension between theories and practices that needs to be worked with. As Cameron (1986) summarises it, 'organisational effectiveness is inherently paradoxical. To be effective, an organisation must possess attributes that are simultaneously contradictory, even mutually exclusive'. These opposites are called tensions (Senge 1997), dilemmas (Hampden-Turner 1990), competing values (Quinn 1988), dialectics (Mitroff and Linstone 1993) and dualities: 'One of the essential postulates of this emerging school of organizational analysis is that such opposites are not "either/or" choices (reminiscent of conventional contingency theory) but dualities that must be reconciled or dynamically balanced' (Evans and Genadry 1999). Different types of tension are discussed in organisational literature, such as relational paradoxes (expressing views and being diplomatic, building relationships with staff while also keeping a distance) and strategic paradoxes (long-term versus short-term planning, flexibility versus goal setting) (Handy 1994). Perhaps the ultimate paradox in relation to meaning is where organisations have to attract the increasing commitment and engagement of the whole person at work by 'providing' more meaning, while much of this meaning (such as strong relationships at work, or satisfaction from truly making a difference) is taken away through meaner and leaner business practice.

Directing action: listening from the whole and responding to the whole

In the final case study in this chapter, Case study 7.5, we look at how a team that was described as dysfunctional work with a consultant to sort out their problems. We'll see how the four quadrants help to identify the elements of an underlying loss of inspiration in a current work situation. Here the consultant, Dave Burton, uses the four pathways to draw out all the key elements of a team's concerns in such a way that at the end they felt heard and had a clear sense of what needed to happen.

Case study 7.5 **Turning a potential bitch session into something much more positive**

The manager of the New Zealand sales team in a multinational organisation had recently resigned and a new manager was appointed from the UK. It was brought to his attention that there were issues in the New Zealand team and he contacted me to ask me if I could find out what these were before he arrived in the country.

In this case, I did not use the model directly with the team. I decided that if I used it upfront they might decide that they were being forced to 'be positive' when they were not ready for that. So I used it indirectly. I asked some simple questions, then organised the answers through the model.

In order to help them focus and clarify each issue I asked these three questions

- What do you call this issue?
- What are its consequences?
- How might you correct it?

As issues arose, I'd map them onto the model. The first issue was that the team were experiencing a lack of leadership and the sorts of things they were saying were, 'Nobody goes into bat for us', 'We don't get any feedback', 'We don't get any recognition', 'We get very few professional development opportunities', and there had been little or no response to their requests for change. The consequence in their eyes was that they were not developing or able to express their full potential and so felt uninspired, which was tragic because these people were naturally high achievers.

Another issue that arose was that they could not use their expertise as they were not allowed to offer any more technical advice than what was printed on the packaging of their products, so their identity as someone who could add value was falling away. The consequence of this was that they were feeling less and less able to be of service and make a difference. They could provide their product but do little more to 'meet the needs of humanity' and this was proving a major and unrecognised de-motivator. As the session went on it became clear that they had a sense of having lost meaning in their work; they had become just order-takers. Yet they all still had a deep passion for their work. It was a highly relationship-oriented business, so unity, shared values and belonging really were important. Unfortunately their team leader's 'hands-off' approach was leaving them feeling uncared for, unimportant and with no sense of being part of anything. Even though I did not make the model visible at any stage, I could completely understand the importance of each of its dimensions when I heard it in their conversation. In this way the model provided me with a very clear framework to hear and validate their concerns. I could say, 'I'm not surprised you feel that way'. The model supported me and stopped me from going into a negative space along with them.

Once we had covered the issues in each of the quadrants they looked at each other and said, 'Well that feels much better'. People had been concerned that it was going to be a bitch session and instead it was tremendously positive. One thing that surprised me was the depth and calibre of these people, once the scope of the conversation broadened and deepened.

So, I wrote up their issues and sent the information to the new manager with the conclusion that 'The leadership provided to the team has not grown in proportion to the team members' own development.'

The team are very hopeful that the new manager will start to bring more and better leadership. However, rather than this being something vague that might resolve their feelings of discontent, they can now clearly represent what it is that they need and, because they understand the deeper reasons behind these needs, do so from a place of strength. At the same time the new manager has a profound place from which to develop his leadership in relation to this team. He can ask, Is my leadership promoting unity, service, expression of full potential and development of self?

Case study 7.5 typifies something that we have noticed time and again in our own work and have had reported to us by numerous people who work with the model. This is that after working with the model for a time it becomes so readily available as a way to make sense of situations that people just pull it out, draw it on the board, draw it in the earth in front of them, or simply describe a couple of specific elements with gestures. Because it is so simple the Holistic Development Model can be easily used in many varied circumstances. When you know it well and have used it for a while, you can use it without further preparation and tailor it to the circumstances in which it seems it would be useful. You can also use just the part that is most valuable at the time.

Designing for the whole

As we said before, organisational practices often become very fragmented over time. Here we look at one practice that was traditionally designed to align the personal need for achievement with the organisational need for growth but that now can be experienced as very empty and meaningless by both manager and employee. We look at how the model assists in designing for the whole human being and monitoring to see that this holistic aspect of a practice is still vital and valuable to those who participate in it.

Performance appraisals: how did they become so fragmented?

Performance appraisals are potentially a useful time for evaluating where one has been, where one is going and how this fits with the objectives of the organisation. It has been argued that they are critical to personal and organisational success. A quick search on the Internet confirms that over time there have been many efforts to perfect the technique. Currently there are at least 11 groups of tried and tested techniques (e.g. behaviourally anchored scales, critical incident methods, management by objectives) on the market; each group carries a wide range of varieties of tests one can choose from. Another quick search also reveals that performance appraisals often go wrong. One website summarises:

> They're every manager's yearly conundrum. In theory, performance reviews make sense. In practice, the exercise borders on the absurd: You have one hour to review a whole year's worth of work, issue a grade usually based on a rudimentary 'satisfaction' scale, and outline goals that you likely won't revisit until next year's meeting. (Korosec 2010)

Korosec goes on to say how the performance review has become a mere 'jumping through the HR hoop'.

If you still have energy to browse further, you will also find that each of the websites that identifies problems aims to fix them by adding another technique. Some of these techniques are indeed quite useful: for example, talking less and asking more questions, having the performance reviews on a more regular basis. But few ask, if we are all doing them, and they are generally a de-motivating experience for both parties, if we just do them to jump through another HR hoop, then what are they for?

Evaluating the extent to which an organisational practice causes personal fragmentation or wholeness

The will to meaning is not dependent on others and the individual can do a performance appraisal against that what he or she identifies to be meaningful. For example, one person does this before he goes to a formal appraisal. He asks himself the questions that we have asked in Chapters 2 and 3 and adds 'How did I enhance/diminish my moral discernment? My creativity? Did I make more or less of a difference this year? Did my presence in my team play a uniting or supportive role?' Another person does this afterwards. For example, she will discern what her boss put emphasis on, such as teaching evaluations, and reclaim them in terms of meaning, asking herself questions such as 'Did I become more or less creative in the process of teaching? Did the comments in the evaluations speak of the difference the learning had made to the students?'

What we have learned

The importance of these approaches is that as individuals we claim back meaning for ourselves. Using the model in this way we restore dignity to ourselves even when the practices in our environment do not support this. In many cases in our workshops an exercise like this helped individuals to see themselves as worthwhile, purposeful and authoritative. From here we can at the very least be constructive with ourselves. It can support us in moving from evaluating ourselves in critical and self-destructive ways to more constructive ones. It can support us in moving from the person who walks away from the performance review with cynicism in her heart to the person who can clearly discern 'well this is me and this is how my boss chooses to do this my performance appraisal at this moment in time'.

Honouring our profound meanings and allowing ourselves to see ourselves as people of purpose gives us a sense of wholeness and integration. This also releases energy. As one participant said, 'This does not bestow wisdom from on high but releases it from within.'

Evaluating a practice through the model in relation to the purpose of the organisation as a whole

At an organisational level we interrogate practices through questions of how they align with the organisational purpose or why, collectively, we are here. Organisations adopt a myriad of purpose statements but these days they would have some reference to what the organisation is contributing. For example, in 2010 Vodafone had on its website:

> As members of the Vodafone family, we are focused on helping achieve the Group's vision—becoming the world's leading mobile communication leader. This means enriching customers' lives and helping individuals, business and communities be more connected in a mobile world.[1]

So in the performance appraisal the emphasis should be on how an employee has contributed to Vodafone as well as how the organisation lived up to its purpose statement from the perspective of the employee. That is, which aspects of that were meaningful to him or her and which aspects made working in the organisation (towards this collective purpose) more meaningful or meaningless. Organisational practices provide ongoing opportunities to evaluate the extent to which what employees find meaningful and how the organisational vision is brought to life are still aligned.

Summary

The experience of meaning is an experience of wholeness, the experience that the different parts of our lives fit together into a coherent

---

1 www.vodafone.co.nz, accessed 13 March 2010.

whole. One of the problems with current organisational life is that it often pulls the individual in conflicting and competing directions and drains everyone's energy. The model helps individuals and organisations to organise, design and direct activities back to a coherent whole. In the next chapter we look at how the model assists in voicing meaning and hence taking meaningful action in organisational contexts.

8

Speaking to meaning within organisational systems

In organisations we use a particular language. It is a language that legitimises business or organisational outcomes and often silences concern for human ways of Being and Doing. Whereas traditionally such language dominated larger commercial organisations, over the past 20 years this business-focused way of talking has also become dominant in not-for-profit organisations such as hospitals and even primary schools. This has made it very hard to speak to human motivations and concerns.

Many people, when they hear these 'business' words spoken, react with 'but this is not why I am here. I did not take this job to contribute to "effectiveness". I do not get out of bed in the morning to be accountable.' However, in organisational conversations it has become hard to voice the deeper reasons why one does choose to be at work. It seems so irrelevant or somehow inappropriate, in any big or small organisational change, for example, to suddenly say, 'but I will miss my colleagues if our teams are reorganised this way' or 'but if I have two minutes less to complete the job, I no longer have time to ask the customer "how is your daughter, how did the operation go", and it is those interactions that make me love my job'. Such comments seem petty or inappropriately personal when the organisation's survival is on the line. Or they seem unprofessional, as if we don't understand the real world of work. And even if it is safe to say them, and they are met with a sympathetic glance, there's no sense that such a comment could in any way halt or affect the proposed change.

Exercise 8.1

▶ **Purpose**

To create awareness of the language used in organisations.

▶ **Instructions**

Think about a recent meeting that you attended in which a change initiative was discussed. This can be anything from the introduction of a new technical system, to a merging of two teams, a change in resource allocation, etc.

Consider some of the points of view and note the sort of language that was used. What words or phrases were used?

What words have been used to try to persuade you that this was a good idea?

What words did you use to persuade others that this was a good idea?

It is most likely that the words used in Exercise 8.1 were ones such as 'goals', 'effective', 'systematic', 'financial pressure', 'successful', 'accountable', 'standards', 'growth' or 'competition'. Or were they phrases such as 'supporting each other', 'doing the right thing', 'making a difference' or 'being creative'? Reflecting back, which words gave you energy? Which words made you tired? Which words seemed to energise others? Which words engaged people, and which disengaged them?

For some people the first set of words makes them feel drained, while the same words inspire others. Some people find the second set of words too airy-fairy and irritating, while others feel as if they are finally talking about what matters and find themselves now able to contribute, whereas before they had nothing to say.

What we have learned

Losing meaning through restrictive language

Time and time again participants discussed how the limited language used in organisations renders the search for meaningfulness invisible. Decisions are usually made in relation to scarcity of resources (particularly in times of economic downturn) and to competition. We may think to ourselves that the organisation's survival in one way or another has been, and always will be, on the line and that there will be no end to this economic imperative. And at some point we may notice that something in us dies a little as we realise there never will be a time when we are welcome to voice our concerns, even if we knew how to do so; or realise that, if we did, it would make no difference.

And yet, at the same time it is recognised (and all organisational best practice and theory agrees, as we see later on in the chapter) that it is important to tap into what intrinsically motivates a human being to flourish and that such human flourishing plays a large part in the success of organisations. However, it seems that this awareness often operates separately from the 'hard' discourse of organisational survival.

For example, at a recent meeting, a group of employees was painted the following picture:

> We expect a 20% decline in international demand for our services and a tightening of the domestic market. Oh, and there is also a push by our CEO for this institution to belong to the world's best. I am going to paint this picture [in somewhat more detail] and would like some suggestions for the strategic direction.

None of the highly educated, highly articulate people in the meeting engaged. The information presented and the challenge set meant little to the employees beyond creating some fear of how they might be affected personally by a possible redistribution of resources. It did not resonate with anything inside them. No one was asked, Why are you here? What is important to you to maintain? What's your vision for our strategic direction? How would you experience your job if we changed from x to y? Initially people challenged the facts somewhat, but quickly they became silent and the dialogue became a manager monologue to convince staff that change was needed although no one was quite sure what purpose such change might serve. From the observed body language this frustrated the manager as much as the staff.

This example shows that it is taken for granted that, somehow, the mantra of 'organisational effectiveness' and 'the bottom line' answers everything, or is so inescapable that there is no need to think or say anything unless it can be framed in alignment with these organisational objectives. This leaves both managers and employees lost for words. We are all disenfranchised from an ability to speak, to use words that we might easily use in other contexts, words that might express compassion for ourselves and for others, words that might open up opportunities to be much more creative, words that might even simply acknowledge 'this is not good but we are in this together and we will make the best of it'.

Increasing meaning through the use of the model

The model makes what is meaningful immediately visible and so helps us to quickly and clearly see the role of meaning in any workplace conversation. Therefore having the model present in some way (in your own mind, on the wall, as part of all organisational decision-making processes) makes it possible to quickly scan for the effects on our humanity of any proposed initiative. So when plans are made, goals are set or changes need to take place, these are evaluated not only against economic objectives but also against the extent to which these enhance or detract from our ability to find meaning.

At the same time, having the model present in any way simply legitimises our humanness. Thus the individual does not need to consider whether he or she is seen to be 'on board' or 'professional' when asking questions about how decisions might affect people. It becomes legitimate to ask questions such as, Will this incentive enable us to work together, or will we be working against each other? Will this plan allow us to be more creative, or will we start treating each other as numbers or outputs? If we go along this route, will we make more or less of a long-term contribution to society?

It becomes legitimate to dwell on these questions for the same length of time that might be spent on some economic questions. We do not suggest that dwelling on such questions always contributes to solutions where economic and human outcomes in the organisation are aligned. But at least there is support for and legitimisation of meaning as a valid topic and focus of workplace conversation and decision-making. Case studies 8.1, 8.2 and 8.3 show how the model was pivotal to people's ability to speak to meaning in their organisations.

Case study 8.1 **Speaking to meaning in a marketing context**

I belong to a local city marketing board. It is a great group of committed people with a wide variety of skills. As I tried to come to grips with the purpose of the organisation I found myself wondering about the focus on retail outcomes. This is totally understandable because our members are largely retailers, but I thought that although it is important to have successful shops, it's not the only thing that makes a city attractive. Having worked with the model for some years I found that it gave me confidence to raise a couple of questions that otherwise I might have been too shy to ask. After about six meetings I asked, 'What is a city if it is not just retail outlets?' We went on to discuss the importance of a city as a place for the community to gather and to create and maintain connections.

Just saying this helped clarify for myself the importance of a city as a site of meaning for people. That's led to my putting my hand up for things like a recent project where we put short poems and phrases on city walls. Thinking through the criteria for selecting the pieces of writing made me think more deeply about the question I had posed. I saw that a city is the place where people have their life experiences and therefore, of course, where they find meaning. It's the place where they think, play, dream, love, contribute, belong, share, support others, work, have children, get old, die, are born, have spiritual experiences and create, as well as shop. So it's helped me understand more deeply the importance of cities beyond just how they are doing economically. I'm still learning how to find effective ways to raise issues of meaning, but the model makes me more confident about keeping going and bringing my voice and insights into the projects in which I am engaged.

Case study 8.2 **Decision-making in a commercial company**

This is a case study of a strategic decision-making group in a commercial organisation. This group had gone through a one-day training session on the model and decided that they would keep the learning visible and actionable by putting a big poster of the model in the meeting room.

The model was quite unobtrusive there. However, during our meetings we regularly found ourselves swinging around in our chairs pointing to various aspects to it. We usually have a lot on the agenda in our meetings so we tend to become quite business-like. The model really assisted us in planning around the important basics, the things that matter most. When we talked about the extent to which we wanted to engage with the union and were well into a discussion about whether this would be efficient or inconvenient, someone immediately pointed towards Unity with Others and said, 'What would the question look like from that perspective?' It shifted the decision-making process and later we welcomed the union onto our premises, and we have worked very constructively with them ever since. When we talked about restructuring someone asked, 'Could we consider restructuring with Expressing Full Potential in mind?' We subsequently could easily discuss how each new position would need to facilitate a growth of skills and that gained us tremendous buy-in. When we looked at leasing a new fleet of cars we looked at one of the things that we had put in the quadrant of Service, which was 'purchasing towards the future we want to create', so it was a small step to include a series of sustainability measures into our purchase plan. When we looked at our own functioning we decided we needed more Being time and started the meetings with a check-in and extended lunch time. Some of these things we might have eventually arrived at in any case as they match our vision and values, but others we would have completely overlooked or not quite have known what questions to ask about them. The shape and structure of the model, the words in it and its easy presence give us a very clear map that allows us to efficiently and naturally integrate deeper questions into our decision-making.

In Case study 8.3, consultant Helena Clayton uses simple questions based on the model and notices how they contribute to profound and enlivening reflection and discussion.

Case Study 8.3 **Women's leadership in the public sector**

I ran the workshop at an international women's leadership conference for the public sector. There were a couple of hundred people there over two days. We called the session 'Putting Spirituality at the Heart of Leadership' and offered it twice. It was oversubscribed and we ran it with a full complement of 50 in each session, so at least half the conference wanted to attend.

I set the model up on the floor before they came in. When they came in I briefly talked through the model, starting with Self and Others, Being and Doing, then the four quadrants, Reality and the inner circle, which I talked about as having meaning that was specific for them, be it 'God' or nature or something else entirely. I invited individual self-reflection on what was their inspiration by asking, 'What does inspiration mean for you? What is your well-spring?' I then invited them to talk about it with somebody. When they talked about it in the larger group some were inspired by their family, or their work, others connected with beliefs or values and others with God or love. We discussed the difference between spirituality and religion. They remarked on how wonderful it felt to be talking about this in a semi-work place.

Then I invited them to move into threes and asked them, 'And if you put this inspiration, whatever it is for you, at the heart of your leadership what difference would it make?'

They thought about this for a while, then discussed it among themselves and finally fed back to the main group. Overwhelmingly, the response was that their leadership would benefit by integrating, even in a small way, their spirit with their work. Again they said how wonderful it was to talk about what was usually squashed, left at the door or not supported in the workplace.

It was a powerful session both times and we got good feedback. It showed me how much you can do in one-and-a-half hours with two questions when the framework you use is simple and profound.

What others have thought

The extent to which we can speak about what matters to us has a major role to play in institutionalising meaning (making it part of the operating consciousness of the organisation) and sustaining meaning (keeping it alive over time). As we have seen, speaking about meaning and its loss at work may at times seem irrelevant or hopelessly naive, but at the same time, once we have agreed that it is OK to speak about meaning it has tremendous impact on decision-making and releases formidable energy.

Many others have thought about how we lose our ability to speak to meaning in organisations. It is a well-identified problem that unfortunately has had few solutions. So what discourses have come to dominate the world of work, and why is this so? Numerous research projects have established that, while higher values are usually stated in mission and vision statements, when it comes to decision-making, economic value is prioritised as the primary guiding principle for action while those aspects that make work meaningful are suppressed or ignored. One explanation of this is that decision-making is set up to serve the vested interests of those in power. Another explanation is that the speed with which decisions are made and are enacted removes any opportunity for reflection, and hence distances the individual from him- or herself (and therefore from what is meaningful). The problem is not with economic efficiency in itself but with its dominance in our discourse, which often excludes the possibility of speaking to human needs. 'This precedence distorts the meaning of effectiveness and simultaneously affects the meaning of human work and human existence' (Morin 1995: 35).

Lisl Klein (2008) gives an account of interviewing someone in an organisation to understand his motivation. She found that listening to meaning required getting through different layers. He began with the obvious:

> 'All I'm interested in is the money. This firm pays well, and that's the only reason I stop here. What a working man wants from his job is the pay packet, and don't let anybody kid you about other fancy notions.'
>
> Half an hour later he was talking about the firm . . . 'Well, you see, when you get a bit older, and the kids are off your hands, and you've paid for the house, and your wife's got a washing machine—you don't need the money so much anymore and you find you start noticing the firm. And by God it can annoy you!'
>
> Half an hour after that he said, 'You know—what I really like is when the machine goes wrong and I'm the only one knows how to put it right.' (Klein 2008: 37-38)

She writes that, like the skins of an onion, a range of meanings exist in most people, and the question is, which of these gets tapped. The model simply helps in quickly tapping this deeper layer of meaning and so supporting people in organisations to voice it. Doing this, Klein notes, is not a matter of being 'nice' to people. It is about being consistent.

> In terms of mental health, it seems to me to be dangerous and damaging that we express one set of values in our private, social, and political lives and a different set of values in our working arrangements, without really intending to. And we need to be more proactive in the way we design these things. (Klein 2008: 260)

At a strategic level, too, it has been recognised that the topics that we can or cannot raise or ask questions about matter, because they focus the direction of strategic enquiry. The model helps us take responsibility for our speaking, knowing that through our language and actions we create the world—one decided by others, or one we choose ourselves. Through language and collaborative interaction, human beings create meaning

The model is effective in voicing what matters most because having it present in the organisation simply legitimises speaking to all its elements. Its presence (on a wall, on the desktop) is not intrusive. It is in a way the smallest organisational intervention that can be made, and yet it has a profound effect, because when we can talk to each other about what is important to us we become alive and make decisions that people can own and commit to.

However, ultimately you need to decide when it is useful to overtly voice the need for human beings to have meaningful work through the model because there are many situations where as one young manager said, 'There is no way on God's earth I could introduce the model in these words to my guys'. At the same time, we want to point out what can potentially be lost if we work covertly with the model—when the structure is used as part of the team leader's or facilitator's framing but is not made clear to the participants. When this occurs participants have nothing to hold onto if meaningfulness is threatened, nor can they support each other because the concept of meaning and its significance has not been openly expressed.

For example, one colleague used the model as a way to frame a two-day workshop but used it reframed in business language. At the end of the two days the team was completely energised with many practical ways forward, but it only took 15 minutes from the CEO, who had not been present, to give his view of things from the business-as-usual framework to destroy all that had been accomplished. We therefore see the value in finding as many ways as you can to openly have conversations about meaningful work. Then if situations arise where meaning is threatened, participants know what they found and what they need to hold on to and can strategise how they might do that. This helps those at the bottom to hold to what is important and be responsible for it rather than rely on their leaders. From whatever position in the organisation we find ourselves, overtly engaging with the human right and need for meaningful work strengthens and empowers everybody concerned.

Bringing the themes of this book together

We complete this section of the book with one final case study. Case study 8.4 is particularly interesting, and perhaps surprising, because it shows that even people we would expect to be able to talk to about what is meaningful can get completely lost in organisations. It shows how they, like all of us, forget to take responsibility for what is most important to them, how they too become fragmented and lose voice. The participants are Anglican priests, within what is of course the very large organisation of the Anglican church. You will find that there are many parallels with other organisations that you have experienced.

On the left-hand side you find the case study as told to us by the facilitator, Steve Tarpery. We suggest you to read this story first, so it may be helpful to cover the right-hand side with a sheet of paper and focus on the left side first.

On the right-hand side we discuss the effect the model has in this situation, or some tips we have learned over the years of working with the model. In doing so, we pick up on several key ideas that we have presented in this book.

Case study 8.4 **Rediscovering meaning in the church**

The facilitator's story

I was asked to design a pilot programme for a group of Anglican priests who were described by a bishop as the 'pissed off and passed over'. The current situation in England at the moment is one where the majority of Anglican clergy are in the early to mid 50s, in roles from which they are unlikely to move. Many are beset by career crisis, mid-life crisis and faith crisis.

We saw two key issues; one is an organisational issue, and the other is a pastoral issue—how does the church support these people in the next stage of their life and ministry? When I was first invited to look at this specific issue, we split it into the two parts: how to reconnect people with a sense of meaning in life generally without them feeling criticised, and how to be realistic in what was available and possible for them.

I worked with a small group of clergy to design a pilot—we called it Celebrating Wisdom—and its purpose was to give people an opportunity to explore the threads of their life that have brought them to here, help them identify the wisdom and gifts they've gathered and how they can think creatively about what can they do with these in the organisation.

Our observations

One of the things that facilitators working with the model have commented on is that because they have internalised elements of the map, such as in this case Inspiration and Reality, they have become more skilled at making those elements present in the conversation. Here that leads to a very realistic but non-judgemental 'this is how it is' problem description. At the same time facilitators remain clear about the constructive focus of the programme and attend upfront to the possibilities for addressing the issues. Thus while the model offers something that might be thought of as 'soft' and even marginal, it is in fact much more real and practical than many management techniques that do not, upfront, build in the obstacles to change.

In work with the church there's a danger in using the term 'spirituality'; people regress into dogma. That is, what they believe is still true to them, but has also become so formulaic that it is no longer alive for them, it no longer drives their daily choices.

The model does not replace or override people's deeply held beliefs. It just aids in voicing these by asking, Is this alive for me? Is this forming a real basis for living? or, Is it just a comforting theory that keeps what is really going on at bay?

Given this, we designed a five-day semi-structured retreat that consisted of things that would be done in a normal church retreat: daily liturgy, use of carefully selected scripture, exercises you would expect in a leadership development programme and some external speakers.

Working with the model does not supersede the practices and skills that the group and the facilitator are already have. Here, the group already has its own useful practices. And the facilitators bring a wide variety of their own skills to the process. These include neurolinguistic programming practices, total quality management practices, open space technology, etc.

The thread was to take people through a life story and to use very simple exercises. In the design of the programme, whenever we did an exercise or activity, we allowed some private time, followed by a small learning/wisdom group in which there was disclosure and discussion. These were facilitated by four clergy that I had trained as facilitators and who had gone through their own version of the course so that they understood it.

It really helps if time and space for Being is an intrinsic part of the programme design.

I did consider using the model almost as the sole exercise for the week, to explore the question of what can I identify that brings me to this point, map my life at this moment, framework for gifts and

The model itself can be introduced, used, and let go of at different times. As you have worked your way through this book, you can trust that you will know when to make it present and when to wisdom and then mapping forward. I didn't do that, it might have been a little bit of cowardice, or that I thought that by using a range of different lenses, for example, a story-telling exercise, that it might be more helpful. However, I did use the model as a core exercise very early in the week. It was the second intervention after a simple life-lines exercise.

let it go, and participants will also have their own input into this.

I knew from my experience of working with the model that of all the tools, interventions and frameworks I've used, this is one that consistently adds value to whatever I'm doing. It's never not worked, it always has an impact and engages everybody. It has rigour, there is a strength to the framework, and sufficient space within that for people to construct their own meaning.

This is the consistent feedback that we are getting from practitioners but the only way you can verify this is simply by finding a place to use it for the first time. In running our workshops about how to use the model, we find it is very useful to end with inviting participants to design an application of it. This way participants move from 'nice to know' to 'let's try this out' and keep using it afterwards.

I always, as I did in this programme, introduce the model very simply and then ask them to physically build the model on the floor; they create it with a rope. In this exercise I asked people to visit each of the elements and record any thoughts, or words they had in relation to it, and leave it on a sticky-note on the floor. I gave them 25 minutes for this.

One of the things we have noticed in our own work and talking to practitioners who use the model is that the model really lends itself to moving around and that this aids participants in grasping it quickly and owning it. In Appendix 1 we will explain that we have created a space where practitioners can share ideas and exercises.

Then I asked them to more explicitly map 'Where am I in my life at the moment?' I asked them to journal, as they moved, sat or stood—some sat at the edge and journalled—for about 30–40 minutes. Then I asked them to find another person and 'walk them through your story. Don't discuss, or interrogate, but just speak it aloud and have it witnessed.' Then witness the other person's. 30 minutes in total, 15 for each person.

Again, it works well if you can design space not only for individual being but also for collective being.

We did this in the evening, so we could sleep on it, and then went into small groups the following morning, with their facilitators, and talked about 'What have you taken from all of that? Having noticed whatever you've noticed, mapped whatever you've mapped, so what?' That was done in small groups, and was private.

We have found that the work with the model is very deep, and it can work to do a short piece on it and move on; it's good to go a bit more slowly and leave time for the whole being to absorb the learning and insights. Sleeping on it, as was done here, is a helpful way to let people integrate the work they are doing. In this case there was no rush for a solution but a gentle allowing of insights to float to the surface overnight.

I have to say the Holistic Development Model was probably the pivotal exercise for the majority of people: both in terms of feedback during the week, and subsequently. The key thing was that it allowed them to explore their beliefs about life more holistically rather than get channelled into a narrow faith belief. It allowed them to take a really good look at the whole of their life. I used it in

The model supports wholeness and integration; this is constantly reinforced by our colleagues and our own experience of working with the model.

terms of how they are now, and then went back to the life-line to look at what they had missed. The framework it gave them then seemed to become a way of thinking that they could use to approach all the other exercises as well. The 'whole picture' concept really took hold.

People readily adopt the model as a guiding frame. It really plants them on their own feet and they can then decide what to do with it.

One of the things that came up for the group as a whole was the feeling of disempowerment that many of them were carrying, an ache that most of them didn't know they had until they talked together about it. It came out in the discussion: the discipline of the church, the discipline of faith, the nature of the role, always being there for other people, and how that left them with a sense that they had lost control of their own lives and that it wasn't OK for them to be asking questions. They had almost lost their personal responsibility for making their own meanings. When we did the exercise with the Holistic Development Model it shifted that.

Once people have identified what is meaningful to them, they want to take action. They no longer want to be passive or negative.

Here the tension between Self and Others and the negative impact of being out of balance for long periods of time is clearly shown and made legitimate in a meaningful context. The model advocates for our bigger selves, so that the need for time for ourself can be understood in this context, rather than in a way that would see this need as selfish.

The tide flows in and out and up and down over a period of time, it's not that you are ever completely balanced, but that you can just notice the movement of the tide. I often suggest that people go back to the model in six months and notice how the tide is flowing now. This always comes across differently from Inspiration and the Reality, because Inspiration and Reality is the framework

As a manager, group member or facilitator you will find your own ways of explaining the various elements of the model. We invite you to use words that work for you and we suggest that, in turn, you invite participants to use the words that work for them. This way the model resonates deeply and has lasting effects because people are much more likely to remember their own insights.

that holds the model and where the fuel comes from the life, the four quadrants are where the tides and winds are taking us at the moment.

There was a noticeable change in the group and they reported back to us that they were now reconnecting with 'we are responsible, we can change things, we are in our charge of our own destiny'.

This shows how people naturally take responsibility when they can firmly stand in their own meaning and see others doing the same.

That was what was so powerful about the week as a whole; a group that collectively had enormous wisdom but one that had not been able to access it; secondly, they suddenly shifted back into what they could do, wanted to do and how they could contribute in different ways. That reconnection was like fires being lit in people.

We may individually know what we believe is the ultimate meaning for our lives. And the clergy in this case could be expected to be more skilled at this then most people. However, what this case so clearly shows is that such knowledge, if not deliberately and actively drawn into our day-to-day working lives, has little impact. The model, by presencing distinct dimensions of meaning, tensions, and the way meaning is always situated in the larger realm between inspiration and reality, helps us to live our daily lives meaningfully rather than just having a belief or theory about this.

The Holistic Development Model started the chain reaction. I can't say exactly how, because it happens deep within people, but the tide changed after working with the model. Over time they had lost connection with their faith. There were some very moving things in the final stage of the

The energy that is released when people are able to connect or reconnect with the meaning at their heart's core is immense, and moving to witness. This energy quite naturally turns into action— action that is grounded in deep and lasting purpose, compared to hyped-up motivation. Our programme about God, their life, what they wanted to be in terms of unity within the church, etc. A few of them had a sense of renegotiating their covenant with their God. Each found something or some things that gave them the platform and released their energy. They re-found their spirit.

experience is that people remain in touch with this heart inspiration—and know what to do if it shifts for any reason—and this continues to support responsible action over time.

The whole programme was so constructive. Now this group is literally banging on the door of two bishops saying, 'You are not using us properly. Here are things we want to do for the church, for you and for us, so use us.'

Here we have the example of people who before the workshop felt burdened and exhausted, now asking for more responsibility because they are now clear about what purpose they want to fulfil and their own contribution to this.

Summary

The model is effective because it is simple and yet able to contain a dynamic complexity, because it is not a technique imposed on participants but a journey made by participants. People usually 'get it' reasonably easily, with varying degrees of involvement, although we have had a few cases where people did not find it easy to work with. It's quick to introduce into a conversation or a presentation and can lead to instant recognition and deep comprehension. People can hold the map in their minds or put it up in various places at work and so easily bring it into daily activities. It is not intrusive, it does not conflict with dearly held world-views and it helps people engage with and act on human issues. Because it is grounded and practical it can be used in ways that do not bring the whole organisation to a halt and, in fact, we have consistently found that it energises people and that they are willing and ready to take responsibility and move to immediate action after working with the model. In Chapter 9 we place the map of meaning in the bigger picture of organising for responsible and sustainable outcomes.

9

Meaningful work at the foundation of the responsibility revolution

Never before have we been asked to be so responsible and so adult at work and in our lives. The effectiveness of this response is tightly interwoven with the manner in which we come together and organise.

> The logic is simple: There is not one item on the global agenda for change that can be understood (much less responded to) without a better understanding of organizations. More than anywhere else, the world's direction and future are being created in the context of human organizations and institutions. Today . . . new spaces have opened for transboundary corporations, networks, nongovernmental organisations (NGOs), regimes, associations, grassroots groups and many others to proliferate. The significance, in many respects, of the relatively small number of decisions made by our nation-state leaders pales in comparison to the billions of decisions made every day by members and leaders of such organisations. (Cooperrider and Dutton 1999: xvi)

At the beginning of this book, we wrote that we cannot arrive at a better understanding of organisations without a more profound understanding of what it is to be human. To be human is to be in search of meaning, energised by what is meaningful to us and able to be our best selves when we are firmly grounded in that which has meaning for us. The organisations of the future therefore need to be constructed so that the awareness of what creates meaningful and worthwhile lives can naturally be part of the billions of decisions made by each of its members and leaders.

In the first part of this book we saw that in our current society it is hard for people to work from the basis of what is meaningful to them. First, because they often find it difficult to articulate, see the whole and act on what is personally meaningful to them, and second, because the organisational systems in which they work regularly lead to silence, fragmentation and disempowerment. Next, we identified ways of organising that more naturally align with who we are as human beings and that allow people to reconnect to what is meaningful to them rather than have this prescribed by the organisation. These ways of organising support people to be grounded in and energised by their own core values and therefore have a strong place from which to contribute to the organisation as well as to challenge its integrity. In this chapter we show why meaningful work needs to be at the foundation of the responsibility revolution.

At a time when existing organisations are taking on new responsibilities, when new enterprises are being created to specifically address social and environmental ills and when the total nature of organising is taking on new forms and new alliances, there exists a truly radical and creative moment in which we can also re-examine and redefine work itself. At the same time, there is a distinct danger that old and defunct organisational practices will be brought to bear on new organisational responsibilities. When we attend forums on sustainability and responsibility we notice how, in the need to be heard and taken seriously, there is much talk about technology, consumer buy-in and efficiency gains and little talk about the members of the organisations that collectively make the billions of decisions that result in responsible and sustainable organisations. We fear that when these old, conservative and top-down organisational frameworks are brought to new organisational challenges the change that will take place will not be fundamental enough. We also fear that old patterns and habits will cripple the organisation's ability to respond as fully and successfully as its members might long to do.

There is an enormous opportunity to redesign work and organisations to better address the demands of the responsibility revolution. But, in order to do so, we believe we must rethink the very patterns of human purpose and interaction that constitute the modern organisation. We suggest that the Holistic Development Model is fundamental to this rethink because it demands that the question of what is a worthwhile life is given a significant place in the design of the organisations of the future.

In this chapter we focus on how working with the Holistic Development Model integrates the need for meaningful work with responsible and sustainable organisational practices. As mentioned in the introduction to the book, the search for meaning is not just another fad; it is a fundamental aspect of the human condition, of human strength and well-being and is at the foundation of choices that sustain our humanity. It is, therefore, fundamental to the responsibility revolution. Responsible work holds great promise for employee commitment. An organisation 'is far more likely to win extraordinary contributions from people when they feel they are working toward a goal of extraordinary consequence' (Hollender and Breen 2010: 25). Such a statement (which we see often in the responsibility and sustainability literature) is based on the premise that organisations that have a purpose beyond profit, such as contributing to environmental sustainability and towards thriving communities, create meaningful work because the purpose of the organisation itself is meaningful. Our research confirms that it is indeed meaningful to people to be able to make a difference within their organisation and towards its major stakeholders. Research participants describe their work as meaningful when they have opportunities to 'give back', 'advocate for the need of others', 'help others to grow', 'replenish the planet', 'help the poor' and 'act with future generations in mind'.

Where organisations link their purpose to making a difference, they attract high-quality workers who have pride in their work and workplaces. At the same time, working towards higher purposes does not, in itself, create meaningful work. Many organisations such as schools, hospitals and NGOs have always worked towards goals of extraordinary consequence, and do attract committed workers because of this. Yet these organisations have far too many unhappy, disengaged or burned-out employees (Maslach and Leiter 1997). Simply changing the purpose of the organisation is not enough to create meaningful work. The *process* of working towards a meaningful goal is equally important.

As we have seen in previous chapters, the extent to which work is meaningful is not just dependent on whether individuals can contribute to transcendent goals, although this is one important part of meaningful work. The extent to which work is meaningful depends also on people's ability to speak about what are and are not meaningful tasks, interactions and outcomes in their day-to-day work; to work in a manner that allows them to bring all parts of themselves to work and be alive to every aspect of existence; to have work in which they are encouraged to act responsibly and constructively towards others as well as themselves; and to have work in which they can be inspired and be hopeful, but also be real and grounded

When the sources of meaningful work are ignored, the reputation of the company can be quickly undermined, even when it has goals of extraordinary consequence. An example of this recently occurred with TNT in the Netherlands. Its mission statement clearly identifies an extraordinary goal: 'we lead the industry by instilling pride in our people, creating value for our stakeholders and sharing responsibility for our world'.[1] TNT has been well regarded for its exemplary sustainability practices. However, a recent drive for efficiency and the effects this had on people working in the organisation became the subject of a prime-time documentary on Dutch television in October 2010. In the documentary, postal workers discuss practices that they experience as dehumanising, such as unreasonable delivery time-lines measured by letters per minute, having lines around their office chairs to indicate the space within which they can and cannot move during the sorting process, and having to circulate recruitment leaflets for part-time workers that will ultimately lead to their own redundancies. They talk about the loss of community and the loss of

---

1 www.tntpost.com/tntpost/mission_vision/index.asp, accessed 25 May 2010.

a sense of self and pride in their work caused by these practices and also how they end up compensating for unrealistic expectations by working longer hours. A team leader also discusses how the meaning of his work is diminished by having to enforce these practices. In a subsequent interview, also on prime-time television, the departing chair of the board of directors acknowledges that mistakes were made. TNT in the Netherlands is not an uncaring company and has made substantial efforts to reemploy workers through recent restructuring. At the same time it works under pressure to provide a substantive return on investment to shareholders.

The point we want to make here is that unless the extent to which we can sustain our humanity at work is central to all decision-making in the organisation, loss of meaning is inevitable and people will still be treated as just another resource in pursuit of a goal, even when the goal is extraordinary. In the previous chapters we have discussed the wide range of causes for this and their substantial effect on worker well-being and engagement. To summarise, people lose connection with their inner selves when organisational values are not lived up to and they find themselves lost in 'moral mazes' at work (Jackall 1988). Technology can alienate people from their work when they no longer have any connection to the end result nor to the contribution of their work (Sennett 2006). The pace of change through which organisations put themselves has caused loss of meaning for employees who can no longer discern what is worthwhile or to what they should commit themselves (Ellsworth 2002). Employees at all levels of the organisation experience bogus empowerment where the objectives towards which employees are 'allowed' to participate are still narrowly defined by others in an environment where there is a lack of trust (Ciulla 2000) and 'far too many people are stifled, constrained, hemmed in, and tied down by bureaucracy and rules that have nothing to do with allowing them to be the best they can be in their jobs' (Carney and Getz 2009: ix). Thus for too many employees the main mode of operation is one of 'muddling through' or 'fighting back', and there is widespread evidence of a shared and pervasive uneasiness in our experience of our daily working life (Scharmer 2007).

Sennett (2006) describes how too much work that diminishes our humanity demands too much sacrifice from society as a whole and is hence not sustainable. The World Health Organisation (WHO) has consistently drawn attention to alarming rates of increasing in stress and depression. While these are of course not only caused by work, it has been interesting to note that the WHO has increasingly been focusing on the relationship between health, well-being and work, and has been drawing attention to the fact that stress is not only (or not even primarily) related to the hours we spend at work. Being shut out from decision-making, dysfunctional workplace relationships and the eroding of time to connect with others all undermine employee well-being and productivity, and also have a high impact on stress.

It is vital that, in the process of creating organisations that are more responsible towards external stakeholders and the environment, we simultaneously take the opportunity to create good work, work that supports people to be their best selves, to make a difference through their work and other parts of their lives, to love and laugh and be their talented and creative selves.

In the following sections we explore how the Holistic Development Model supports a sustainable alliance between employee commitment and purpose beyond profit. We pick up our now very familiar three outcomes that come from working with the model: responsibility, wholeness and voicing, and show the significance of each of these for organising towards responsible social and environmental goals.

Connecting personal meaning and purpose beyond profit

Getting off the soapbox: sharing responsibility

In Chapter 6 we discussed how the map of meaning connects individual meaning to organisational purpose. We saw that the model is useful in creating a strong connection between individual motivation and organisational purpose because it supports building organisational purpose, mission and vision from the bottom up while also building strong relationships within the organisation, which is a first step in changing the organisation at a profound level.

While the responsibility and sustainability literature clearly recognises how important it is that values are widely shared, far too much guidance on how to create purpose and achieve buy-in is still built on old assumptions about the management of human beings. It still suggests that first the CEO (or a small appointed group) need to become clear on purpose and values, that they next need to get onto a soapbox and ensure that everyone buys into this purpose, and that this process needs to be tightly controlled because otherwise it becomes unwieldy and fails to lead to action. Yes, as Senge points out, this is often counterproductive: 'Sustainability champions . . . frequently end up pushing their ideas into the organization. They achieve marginal impact at best and risk alienating a great many people who might otherwise be open to becoming engaged themselves' (Senge 2010: 209).

When you work with the Holistic Development Model, you work from a fundamentally different premise about what it is to be human and this leads to fundamentally different practice:

- The organisation can only be committed to the extent that individuals within it are committed. We saw earlier how effective it is to use a two-step process when deciding what the organisation stands for. Individuals first need to reconnect to what is meaningful to them before they can connect to, and take responsibility for, the organisational purpose. The advantages of starting with the personal and working out from there to the organisation are described in depth in Chapter 6. That chapter also describes why it is important that all individuals in the organisation, regardless of role or rank, are part of the whole process

- The model offers a structure for moving from what is individually meaningful to statements that are collectively shared. It does so in a manageable way because it allows you to work with what is universal and therefore takes meaningfulness out of the subjective and individualistic to where it is real and shared. At the same time it allows for the use of your own language and world-view and hence connects the individual in a powerful way to the bigger meanings and principles on which members of the organisation can collectively act, as described in depth in Chapter 3

- A co-created organisational purpose has collective responsibility built into it. Therefore it is more straightforward to generate the practical expression of that purpose because people are already deeply committed to it. They know what needs to happen, and they share a language about this. This leads to immediate and efficient action

- The model is a simple and constant reminder that legitimises asking questions about how the myriad of decisions made every day by everyone in the organisation affects people's ability to be fully their best. People who are firmly grounded in their own meaning challenge themselves, each other and the organisation to practice what is being preached. This supports ongoing commitment to the purpose of the organisation

- The model is also a constant reminder that it is legitimate for the stakeholders of the organisation to ask questions about what the organisation does that helps human flourishing. We discuss this in the next section

All evidence points towards the need for widely shared ownership of the organisational purpose and the specific values that might flow from it. For example, Rosabeth Moss Kanter (2009) in her study on multinationals found that in companies in which values are widely shared and collectively owned, employees make better decisions, collaborate more effectively and react to opportunity (and crises) more efficiently.

Integrity between actions and systems: working from wholeness

In Chapter 4 we saw how the Holistic Development Model enables us to see all elements of meaning together as well as how they relate to each other. We saw how this allows us to experience inner order and integrity. In Chapter 7 we described how fragmentation of organisational practices and disconnection from Self and Others leads to loss of meaning and commitment as people feel pulled in different directions. We showed how the model is useful in creating not only a sense of shared purpose but also that it helps to create internally integrated systems and practices to support this purpose. Here we show how the model aids in creating integrity between internal and external organisational values and systems. The need for integrated systems is consistently pointed out in the responsibility and sustainability literature but nevertheless seems to currently elude many organisations striving for responsible outcomes. As Lynn Sharp Paine (2003: 167) writes:

> Innumerable companies have spawned mini-bureaucracies to administer various special programs—for ethics, diversity, compliance, the environment and so on . . . Far too many of these programs are peripheral and largely self-contained activities with little connection to the company's main operating systems . . . success in meeting the new performance standard will require something much more comprehensive and fundamental.

The drive for responsible, sustainable organisations can lead to greater fragmentation and disconnection, and to greater cynicism when it becomes another unfilled promise. However, the new organisational responsibilities of the organisation provide a unique opportunity to create integrated internal and external systems that are fully integrated and build integrity into every aspect of organising.

The human need to make a difference can be expressed naturally in an organisation that works towards purposes beyond profit. This, as we have seen earlier is largely fulfilled by organisations with purpose beyond profit, as long as the process of organising fully acknowledges and works with the human need for meaning. We show below how this works for each of the other dimensions of the model.

The human need for unity can be developed to a greater extent when the organisation is in unity with its stakeholder community

Where members of the organisation have not experienced unity internally, stakeholder engagement can become yet one more independent activity that increases a sense of fragmentation. When people cannot listen to each other in the organisation, nor collaborate, we cannot expect them to have the open, inclusive mindset of world citizenship required by full stakeholder engagement. When an organisation is already designed around meaningful work, the human need for Unity with Others can naturally expand through corporate social and environmental responsibility because all members of the organisation already experience how meaningful it is to work together, share values and belong. They naturally solve problems and create opportunities through working together and sharing values with their stakeholders and having a sense of belonging to the wider community. They know the importance of standing up to bullies, including stakeholder bullies. They experience the energy of shared meaning when they work together with customers to create more useful products or services; or when their conversations about values translate into consumer choices. Similarly, work can be infused with meaning through working together with a rich tapestry of stakeholders such as suppliers, communities, NGOs and governments. Thus, in an organisation in which people already experience Unity with Others and are skilful at creating unity, stakeholder engagement naturally aligns with meaningful work and thus draws on the commitment, focus and energy that meaning releases.

The human need to develop the inner self is naturally met in an organisation that is responsive to ethical concerns

Ethics management can become a narrow duty or a tightly controlled activity that increases a sense of fragmentation and depletes employee energy. For example, when members of the organisation have an internal code of ethics that is not a living document they are unlikely to work together on an ongoing basis with external stakeholders to put processes in place that work towards ethical standards. When there are no reflective practices in the organisation to, for example, identify deadlines or promotion practices that lead to unethical behaviour internally, it is unlikely that members of the organisation can identify how the extent to which they put pressure on suppliers to meet targets can create unethical behaviour. Members of the organisation can naturally Develop Their Inner Selves to a greater extent in an organisation that has high ethical standards. With regard to justice, for example, they will enquire into work conditions throughout the supply chain, asking, What is it that we do that enables others to do the right thing? An organisation that already supports all its members to Develop Their Inner Selves and ask the right questions naturally embraces responsible and sustainable practices, through creating meaningful work.

The human need to express one's full potential is expressed naturally in organisations that explore new opportunities and technologies as well as new ways of thinking and acting

Innovation management can just become another independent activity that becomes disconnected from the human need to create and achieve. If the unique talents of employees have been stifled inside the organisation, they are unlikely to see a use for them in activities external to the organisation. If they have had little freedom to look for creative solutions inside the company, they are unlikely to find creative solutions to difficult problems, such as finding new ways of sourcing products locally. When members of the organisation have not been supported to be creative nor experienced a sense of achievement within the organisation, they cannot be expected to arrive at the creative solutions that are required to create a better world. In an organisation that is already designed on the basis of what makes work meaningful, members of the organisation get more opportunities to Express Their Full Potential in relation to the expanding social and environmental responsibilities of the organisation. Innovation is very important to responsible organising and to sustainable practice. It is a counterweight to business as usual. Thus an organisation that has already developed a culture and practices that support creativity naturally expands this to create a larger circle of innovation. In *Hybrid Organisations*, Boyd *et al.* (2009) surveyed companies with purpose beyond profit and found that 83% of these claimed to have had notable innovations relating to product or service. These innovations spanned an enormous range from creating sustainable technology, to finding new ways to source products locally, to co-creating new products with suppliers, to finding innovative ways of serving customers who need the product or service but have not traditionally been able to afford it. Creativity and the sense of achievement that comes from seeing new ideas working is essential in imagining and bringing about a better world and naturally flows from the creation of meaningful work.

The human need for balance is developed naturally in organisations that develop sustainable work practices in which all elements of the model can be expressed

For responsible and sustainable organisations the relationship to time, often expressed in a demand for instant results and tight deadlines, is being rethought at a fundamental level. Responsible organisations by their very nature need to balance long-term effects with immediate results. Several companies now match the pressures of the marketplace with patient capital as a way to get back some control over time. Thus, as the responsible organisation supports meaningful work internally by creating the right balance between Doing and Being through creating relief from goal-directedness and busyness, it also learns to create relief from external market pressures and regularly take time out to reflect on the bigger picture. Moreover, in such organisations it is recognised that people who have meaningful lives outside work do not only experience greater well-being and have more energy to bring to work, but are also more likely to ask questions about the responsibility of the organisation towards their families, communities and environment, as they feel more of a connection to these. Similarly organisations that are already skilful internally at having discussions about the needs of self and others will also be more skilful at addressing the balance between the needs of the organisation itself and that of its stakeholders. For example, we hear of organisations that find it difficult to have conversations about when and how much to give away, for it is hard to determine how much is enough. Yet it is legitimate to ask questions about the right balance between the needs internal to the organisation and those external to it and such discussions are a natural part of creating meaningful work.

In responsible organisations the inspiration that is derived from the huge opportunities to make a difference naturally flows because these organisations act on a positive and hopeful view about the future of humanity and the planet

At the same time, the human need to be real also expresses itself naturally in such organisations because they can face up to where they fall short. They can humbly and hopefully hold inspiration and reality together in all decisions and conversations that take place on a daily basis. People working in organisations that cannot face Reality cannot possibly be expected to create transparent organisations. Goodpaster (2000: 197) writes that

> Companies that have the courage to articulate their core values and to communicate them clearly to insiders and outsiders are inviting the charge of hypocrisy on a regular basis. None of us is immune to observations of disconnection between aspiration and action.

- Reality is seen as an opportunity for responsible and sustainable organisations: 'You can view unrealistic expectations as a nuisance to be managed or you can view them as a vaccination against complacency' (Hitchcock and Willard 2006: 8). To create such opportunities, a culture of organisational humility is required that manifests as a willingness of all members of the organisation to be self-critical about gaps between their espoused core values and practice. Taking responsibility between Inspiration and Reality is addressed in Chapter 6 and there we showed its connection to meaningful work. If the organisation consciously or unconsciously attempts to portray itself without flaws, and this is inconsistent with the employee experience of organisational reality, this creates a sense of meaninglessness (Schwartz 1995)

- Members of the organisation cannot possibly be expected to be 'inspired' when a disconnect between the internal practices of the organisation and its external aspirations and portrayal of itself is ignored. When external stakeholders, including customers, see this conflict they too become cynical, withdrawing their support for the organisation by not purchasing their products. On the other hand, when organisations align cultures and systems with what is already deeply meaningful to people, the energy, positivity, commitment and resourcefulness provided by meaningful work supports all members of the organisation to achieve extraordinary goals

There are enormous opportunities for meaningful work in organisations when the internal and external parts of these organisations are connected and operate in ways that complement and extend the interrelatedness of all components. This interconnection therefore is central to connecting each member of the organisation to its goals. Where this is not the case, even the drive for responsibility and sustainability can lead to greater fragmentation, disorder and loss of integrity, all of which disconnect the members of the organisation from its goals. Fragmentation (and the loss of responsibility and engagement it leads to) cannot be managed through adding more layers of bureaucracy. What is required at this fundamental level of meaning is a conscious awareness of the relationship between patterns internal to the organisation and those external to it and putting systems into place where these can strengthen each other. All the dimensions of meaningful work in the Holistic Development Model are therefore not just nice to have, they are essential to responsible and sustainable organising because attending to each of the elements of the model builds conscious awareness, skills and ongoing commitment to being responsible. At the same time, the responsibility revolution enables each of these meanings to be more fully expressed.

Shouting to the rooftops: alternative ways of doing business

In Chapter 3 we discussed how the Holistic Development Model helps individuals to have words to articulate what is meaningful to them and how this also enhances collective conversations about the bigger questions about what constitutes a life well lived. In Chapter 8 we discussed how this aids people to articulate what is (and is not) of permanent value in these times of rapid organisational change.

Here we address how an organisation that is genuinely engaged in corporate responsibility and in taking care of the environment has to make decisions about how best to use its public voice.

A responsible organisation needs to be able to lift its contributions to the public conversation above the economic rationale alone. It needs to speak to who we are as human beings, what makes us well and what makes us happy, to speak beyond purely self-interested conceptualisations of mankind. One of the major contributions of the sustainability movement is that it challenges the view that 'once we have the economy sorted we can attend to other things such as social conditions or the environment'. It is a movement that questions the very foundations and purposes of our lives. Responsible organisations have a responsibility to voice alternative frameworks because these give us choices in conceiving futures in which human beings, and the communities in which they live, thrive sustainably.

People cannot thrive when they feel concerned about the future, when too many people around the globe are suffering, when they know that many natural resources such as fish and forests may no longer be available to their children and when they doubt that our planet will sustain us. In addition, as we have already discussed, people feel very ambivalent about the many ways in which work, and the way it is organised, currently affects their lives. Yet as we saw in Chapter 8, it is difficult to speak to alternative frameworks, even when the company aims to become more socially responsible or sustainable. As Lars Kolind, former CEO of Oticon and Grundfos, says:

> With both Oticon and Grundfos, I faced a lot of social and environmental challenges, as well as major issues about our product focus. When I look back upon the decisions that I've lobbied for, they've been on behalf of the environment and social issues—even though if I had been asked at the time what was most important, I probably would have said to make money. As it turns out my focus was and is a very good basis for strategy—and we're making money . . . I can see that I have a much stronger interest in non-financial issues and I am happy that they turned out to make financial sense. I know what I want but I cannot always express why. That can be a problem when you deal with the board and all of the financial guys, because it is hard for them to accept anything just based on 'knowing

> it is the right decision'. They are so used to focusing on
> rational arguments based on short-term economic results.
> (Pruzan and Pruzan Mikkelsen 2007: 131)

Clearly it is important to speak wisely and with an awareness of
the importance of timing when we speak out. But we also need to
ask, How does the voice of organisations break free from this limited
framework? How does it speak consistently across its community of
stakeholders, including its shareholders? How does the organisation
transparently acknowledge who benefits by its existence? How does
the voice of the organisation encourage democracy, participation
and citizenship? How does the organisation authentically speak in
a way that gives all organisational members and the world's citizens
hope? We are increasingly hearing business voicing such questions.
For instance, Ray Anderson, Founder and Chairman of Interface,
asks what the business case is for human extinction,[2] just one example of effectively questioning the status quo.

Trusting the human need for meaning

This whole book is based on the premise that human beings have
a need for meaning and that meaning is for them a natural place
from which to act. We want to reiterate that this is the case not only
in smooth waters but also, and very much so, when they face challenges, be they those of climate change, a desperately needed political or social change or natural disasters.

We have had the chance to see first-hand how people faced with
challenges respond by doing what is meaningful. While writing this
book during the ongoing earthquakes and aftershocks in Christchurch, we have observed that people have naturally sought meaning.
We saw how they, at a point when they were quite literally shaken to
the core of their being, brought each of the dimensions of the model
to their actions and sense-making. They did so by serving others, and
we often hear people say something like, 'I have to help otherwise

2 www.interfaceglobal.com/getdoc/98a03a4b-65c0-4a61-8984-
   bc6777b90819/Ray-Watch.aspx, accessed 8 July 2011.

I'll go mad.' People from all walks of life—students, farmers, sports, community and religious groups—all came with their shovels and wheelbarrows to clean the streets of silt and sewerage. The (often new immigrant) carers for the elderly walked across a dangerous city to be with their patients. The road-workers toiled day and night and commented when interviewed on radio how great it was to be able to do something and how each pothole they filled made life easier for already distracted drivers. People know that relationships are central to getting through this time. Businesses started working together and, for example, a greengrocer moved in with the coffee shop and a bookshop moved in with the local medical centre. Neighbours meet for meals. People speak to each other on the streets. In the huge catering organisation set up to support all volunteer workers throughout the city, the cooks and cleaners were told to stop work every hour because 'it is important that we get to know each other'.

People express their creativity and need for achievement by, for example, the creative way they have decorated empty spaces where buildings have been demolished and have painted the temporary cladding on their houses. They have brought skills honed over the years to new heights: for example, men have stabilised the cranes so that they continue to work even during the aftershocks.

It is also a time when people go deeply into themselves to find the resources they need. For example, the builders who, although under great stress, are kind and caring as they dismantle people's homes; the teachers who have learned to manage their own fears so that they don't frighten the children when aftershocks occur; and all the people who are honest and trustworthy, enabling everyone to more easily share their resources. For example, the priest who said to volunteers, 'You'll find the van with everything you need in it around the front, the keys are in it. Just bring it back when you've finished. And thank you.' And of course they brought it back.

We also hear the numerous voices of ordinary people, who along with professionals in post-disaster planning, recognise what is happening and write to the local papers admonishing those in positions of power to please recognise these natural ways of being human in the next stage of the planning. Of course, there are those making use of the situation for their own ends, and the chaos and danger of many situations demands quick and decisive top-down action. Organising and organisations are necessary and at the same time, here as everywhere, the challenge for those rebuilding the city will be to integrate this rich and natural human energy into forms that give it space, and support it to flourish.

Conclusion

We consistently find that systems that are based on what it is to work meaningfully are, by definition, systems that are naturally aligned. Thus the Holistic Development Model provides a simple but very helpful vantage point from where to assess and achieve integration of organisational practices.

We need humanity to be capable of more responsible action than it has collectively achieved to date. We believe that by placing the Holistic Development Model at the centre of our thinking about organisations we have a reliable map to lead us into the future. It is based on enduring sources of meaning, tested and proven to be relevant in today's world. The model is grounded at a time when we very much need to keep our feet on the ground. It requires us to face and deal with reality—which is essential—while keeping our connection to the inspiring possibility of what humanity can achieve. It is balanced, when the pressures of the challenges ahead are most likely to tip us into fear and therefore loss of balance, with all the dangers inherent in that. It argues for a unified view of humanity at a time when we most need to practically work with all the people in the world. It supports us in seeing the meaningfulness in each person, to relate to them and ourselves as meaningful and of value, when we most need to respect and value each other. It requires each of us to take equal and full responsibility when it is vital that all people do so. It helps us in knowing ourselves and so helps us attain and retain increasing awareness of ourselves and others. It supports us in being peaceful and mature, and no matter what challenges lie ahead, it calls us to live rich and meaningful lives.

Meaningfulness speaks of the depth of humanity and it is at this deep level that the potential for a new future lies.

Appendix 1
Joining us in creating more meaningful working lives

This book has arisen out of 15 years of ongoing work with the Holistic Development Model. The book represents ordering our findings into a map of meaning, and then offering that into the world: to you, in fact. It has been wonderful work to be involved in and also incredibly challenging. To try to put words to the inner world of meaning has been a long and confronting task.

Where does that leave us as authors? Where does it leave us as a group of committed practitioners? And where does it leave you? What comes next?

In this appendix we discuss our vision for our work, our hopes for the future and how you can become part of this future.

We would not have embarked on this work if we did not think that it had the potential to contribute something of great value to our fellow human beings. The further we have progressed with it, the more value we have been able to see in it. We hope that has also been your experience in reading this book and in doing the exercises. Before we go any further, we invite you to pause a moment and think over the impact this book has had on you. As we have done throughout the book we invite you to do so using Exercise A.1.

Exercise A.1

> Notice what uses for the model have arisen as you have read it.
>
> Think about where it might already be influencing how you think about things.
>
> Notice what vision you have for the ideas in this book.
>
> How do you see them developing in your life? In your workplace, in your community, in your industry, in your country?
>
> What role do you see yourself playing in this?
>
> What support do you need to do this?
>
> How can we help?

These questions are based on the responses that we have already received from people who have read the manuscript and done our workshops. Many have invented new uses for the model and a number have made it a key aspect of their work. Some of them are the group of supportive practitioners that we have mentioned numerous times in the text. They asked us for this book, and it was largely spurred on by their demand and support that we have written it. They also talked about wanting a community of practitioners and ways that they could get together with others who use the model. We see this as something we would love to be part of creating and supporting.

So, what do we envision?

Our vision is that the Holistic Development Model will be available in all parts of the world, so that all human beings who want access to the model can have it. Since it comes from the wisdom of ordinary people, we simply wish it to return to ordinary people. There are a number of ways that we think things might continue from here.

First, use our **website** to learn more about ways to work with the model:

www.holisticdevelopment.org.nz

On it you will find three main areas of interest: using the model, the services we offer and future development of the model and work to do with it.

Using the model

Copies of the model—free

We are happy for you to download copies of the model and use it. We offer two versions: Appendix 2 has just the names of the key elements on it and Appendix 3 just the outline of the model; both are useful for the exercises in the book. We request that you use both of these with the copyright attributed to Marjolein Lips-Wiersma.

Brief explanation of the model—free

On the website there is a brief explanation of each element of the model, which again we are happy for you to download and use. Again, we request that you leave the wording as it is and the copyright at the bottom of the pages.

We will investigate any breach of copyright. This is out of a desire to maintain the academic rigour of the model and ensure the quality of the work remains undiluted.

List of certified practitioners using the model

As you can see from reading the book, the quality of the work done with the model is in large measure dependent on the people who facilitate or lead the work. The list covers the countries around the world and the people in them who are certified practitioners with links to their website or contact details. While this list is currently small we envisage it growing. In the countries where there is no one presently working using the model you might be inspired to be the person to start.

Training and Certification Programme

We are happy to certify people who want to use the model. To do this you will need to take a course with us that will provide a thorough introduction to the model and train you to use the model effectively. Please contact us if you want to do this training.

Community of practitioners

This list will also provide you with information of people in your area with whom you can form a Users Group. We have found it so wonderful over the years to have others who are working with the model, to share with and learn from, that we suggest that you set up the same for yourself.

Services we offer

Our expertise in the Holistic Development Model

Please contact us if you would like us, or one of our certified practitioners to contribute in any of the following ways:

- Public speaking

- Facilitating workshops on the Holistic Development Model

- Specific interventions and organisational consulting where meaning is important

- Working with policy-makers where meaning is important

- Being part of think-tanks

- Facilitation of topics in which meaning is significant

Copies of academic papers and articles

These will be uploaded onto our website as we write them.

Blog

We have a blog on our website so we can keep you up to date with new developments in our work, workshops, writing and any other exciting news.

Future development of the Holistic Development Model

New applications of the Holistic Development Model

The website will also contain a place where we list applications of the model that we think would be valuable to have available but aren't able to do ourselves. Examples of these include:

- Curriculum development
- Architecture and meaningful living and meaningful work
- Community development using the model
- Healing and meaning
- Sustainability and human meaning
- Public policy and human meaning

Research

We have founded our work on rigorous research and believe it is vitally important that future developments of the Holistic Development Model are thoroughly researched. Consequently we invite Honours, Masters and PhD students to do future research on the model. So, please contact us if you are interested in this.

Forthcoming books and downloads

We will provide information about forthcoming books that we are writing, or that others are writing about the model. We are also in the process of writing downloads on special topics for which you will need to pay a small fee:

- Planning Meaningful Retirement
- Meaning and the Arts
- Parenting using the Holistic Development Model
- Curriculum Development

- Meaning and Healing
- Career Development
- Leadership

Online courses

We are developing a range of online courses and would be interested to know what topics would be of most interest to you.

In conclusion

Finally, and most of all, we want you to use the model. We have done this work to offer something that is useful to others. It is therefore important to us that these ideas are used by as many people as possible. From the very beginning we have been delighted when workshop participants, leaders, managers and employees immediately began to use the Holistic Development Model in one way or another. We are looking forward to hearing about new uses of the model and are eager to try them out ourselves, so please contact us.

We have always acknowledged the passion and wisdom of the ordinary people, like you and us, whose struggles and insights have provided the raw data that formed the foundations to this map of human meaning. We look forward to continuing to work with you.

Appendix 2
The Holistic Development Model™ with key elements

The Holistic Development Model™

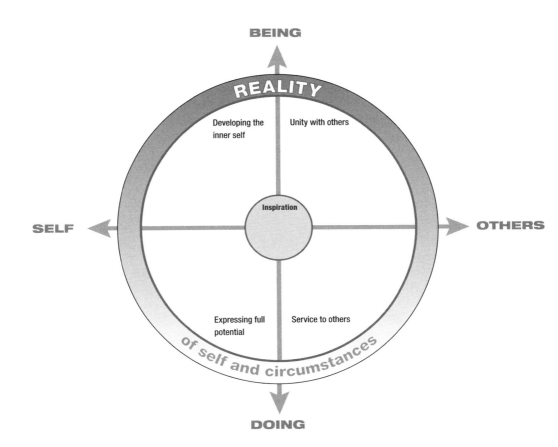

Appendix 3
The Holistic Development Model™ blank version

The Holistic Development Model™

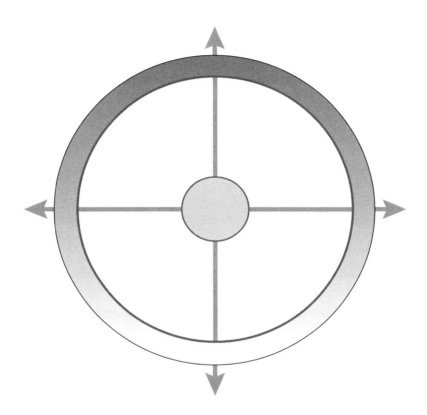

Appendix 4
Certified practitioners and their contact details

New Zealand

Dave Burton
www.potential.co.nz

Patricia Greenhough
www.lifetimelearning.co.nz

Marjolein Lips-Wiersma
www.holisticdevelopment.org.nz

Lani Morris
www.holisticdevelopment.org.nz

United Kingdom

Robin Burgess
www.robinburgessolpd.co.uk

Helena Clayton
helenajclayton@gmail.com

Sue Howard
www.holisticleadership.co.uk

Steve Tarpery
www.humandimensions.co.uk

References

Angyal, A. (1965) *Neurosis and Treatment: a Holistic Theory* (New York: Wiley).

Ashforth, B.E., and D. Vaidyanath (2002) 'Work Organizations as Secular Religions', *Journal of Management Inquiry* 11.4: 359-70.

Bakan, D. (1966) *The Duality of Human Existence: Isolation and Communion in Western Man* (Boston, MA: Beacon Press).

Berry, T. (1988) *The Dream of the Earth* (San Francisco: Sierra Club Books).

Block, P. (2003) *The Answer to How is Yes: Acting on What Matters Most* (San Francisco: Berrett-Koehler).

—— (2008) *Community: The Structure of Belonging* (San Francisco: Berrett-Koehler).

Boyd, B., N. Henning, E. Reyna, D.E. Wang and M.D. Welch (2009) *Hybrid Organizations: New Business Models for Environmental Leadership* (Sheffield, UK: Greenleaf Publishing).

Briskin, A. (1998) *The Stirring of Soul in the Workplace* (San Francisco: Berrett-Koehler).

Buber, M. (1970) *I and Thou* (trans. W. Kaufman; New York: Touchstone).

Cameron, K.S. (1986) 'Effectiveness as Paradox: Consensus and Conflict in Conceptions of Organizational Effectiveness', *Management Science* 32.5: 539-53.

Caproni, P. (1997) 'Work/Life Balance', *Journal of Applied Behavioral Science* 1.33: 46-56.

Carney, B.M., and I. Getz (2009) *Freedom, Inc.: Free Your Employees and Let Them Lead Your Business to Higher Productivity, Profits, and Growth* (New York: Crown Business).

Casey, C. (1999) 'Come and Join Our Family: Discipline and Integration in Corporate Organizational Culture', *Human Relations* 52.2: 155-78.

Chalofsky, N.E. (2010) *Meaningful Workplaces: Reframing How and Where We Work* (San Francisco: Jossey-Bass).

Ciulla, J.B. (2000) *The Working Life: The Promise and Betrayal of Modern Work* (New York: Three Rivers Press).

—— (2004) *Ethics, the Heart of Leadership* (London: Praeger Publishers, 2nd edn).

Cooperrider, D.L., and J.E. Dutton (1999) *Organizational Dimensions of Global Change: No Limits to Cooperation* (Thousand Oaks, CA: Sage Publications).

—— and D. Whitney (2005) *Appreciative Inquiry* (San Francisco: Berrett-Koehler).

Costea, B., N. Crump and K. Amiridis (2008) 'Managerialism, the Therapeutic Habitus and the Self in Contemporary Organizing', *Human Relations* 61.5: 661-85.

Cottingham, J. (2003) *On the Meaning of Life* (Hove, UK: Psychology Press).

Court, D. (2004) 'The Search for Meaning in Educational Research', *Academic Exchange Quarterly* 8.3: 283-87.

Dewey, J. (2010) 'The Mania for Motion', in H. Rosa and W.E. Scheuerman (eds.), *High-speed Society: Social Acceleration, Power and Modernity* (University Park, PA: Pennsylvania State University).

Drucker, P.F. (1994) *The Age of Discontinuity* (New Brunswick, NJ: Transaction Publishers).

Ellsworth, R. (2002) *Leading with Purpose: The New Corporate Realities* (Stanford, CA: Stanford University Press).

Evans, P., and N. Genadry (1999) 'A Duality-Based Prospective for Strategic Human Resource Management, Research and Theory', in J.B. Shaw, P.S. Kirkbride, L.D. Dyer and J. Boudreau (eds.), *Strategic Human Resources Management: An Agenda for the 21st Century* (Stamford, CT: JAI Press).

Frankl, V. (1963) *Man's Search for Meaning: An Introduction to Logotherapy* (New York: Washington Square Press).

Goodpaster, K.E. (2000) 'Conscience and Its Counterfeits in Organizational Life: A New Interpretation of the Naturalistic Fallacy', *Business Ethics Quarterly* 10.1: 189-201.

—— (2007) *Conscience and Corporate Culture* (Malden, MA: Blackwell Publishing).

Gruen, A. (1999) *Heaven Begins Within You: Wisdom from the Desert Fathers* (New York: Crossroad Publishing).

Hampden-Turner, C.M. (1990) *Corporate Culture: From Vicious to Virtuous Circles* (London: Hutchinson/Economist Books).

Handy, C. (1994) *The Age of Paradox* (Boston, MA: Harvard Business School Press).

Havel, V. (2004) 'An Orientation of the Heart', in P.R. Loeb (ed.), *The Impossible Will Take a Little While: A Citizen's Guide to Hope in a Time of Fear* (New York: Basic Books).

Hermans, H.J.M., and E. Hermans (1995) *Self-narratives: The Construction of Meaning in Psychotherapy* (New York: Guilford Press).

Herzog, W., and P. Cronin (2002) *Herzog on Herzog* (London: Faber & Faber).

Hitchcock, D., and M. Willard (2006) *The Business Guide to Sustainability: Practical Strategies and Tools for Organizations* (London: Earthscan).

Hollender, J., and B. Breen (2010) *The Responsibility Revolution: How the Next Generation of Business Will Win* (San Francisco: Jossey Bass).

hooks, b. (2009) *Belonging: A Culture of Place* (New York, NY: Routledge).

Howard, S., and D. Welbourn (2004) *The Spirit at Work Phenomenon* (London: Azure Press).

Jackall, R. (1988) *Moral Mazes: The World of Corporate Managers* (San Francisco: Jossey Bass).

Jackson, I., and J. Nelson (2004) *Profits with Principles* (New York: Doubleday).

Kanter, R.M. (2009) *Supercorp: How Vanguard Companies Create Innovation, Profit and Growth* (New York: Crown Business).

Klein, L. (2008) *The Meaning of Work: Papers on Work Organization and the Design of Jobs* (London: Karnac Books).

Korosec, K. (2010) 'Why You're Doing Performance Reviews All Wrong', www.brittenassociates.com/articles.htm, accessed 6 July 2011.

Krishnamurti, J. (1973) *The Awakening of Intelligence* (London: Victor Gollancz).

Lips-Wiersma, M.S. (2000) 'The Spiritual Meaning of Work' (PhD thesis, University of Auckland).

—— (2002) 'Analysing the Career Concerns of Spiritually Oriented People: Lessons for Contemporary Organizations', *Career Development International* 7.7: 385-97.

—— and C. Mills (2002) 'Coming out of the Closet: Negotiating Spiritual Expression in the Workplace', *Journal of Managerial Psychology* 17.3: 183-202.

—— and L. Morris (2009) 'Discriminating Between "Meaningful Work" and the "Management of Meaning"', *Journal of Business Ethics* 88.3: 491-511.

—— and S. Wright (forthcoming) 'Measuring the Meaning of Meaningful Work', *Journal of Vocational Behavior*.

Marshall, J. (1989) 'Re-visioning Career Concepts: A Feminist Invitation', in M.B. Arthur, D.T. Hall and B.S. Lawrence (eds.), *A Handbook of Career Theory* (Cambridge, UK: Cambridge University Press): 275-91.

Maslach, C., and M.P. Leiter (1997) *The Truth about Burnout: How Organizations Cause Personal Stress and What to do About It* (San Francisco: Jossey Bass).

McAdams, D.P. (1992) 'Unity and Purpose in Human Lives: The Emergence of Identity as a Life Story', in R.A. Zucker, A.I. Rabin, J. Aronoff and S. Frank (eds.), *Personality Structure in the Life Course: Essays on Personality in the Murray Tradition* (New York: Springer): 323-75.

McKenzie, J. (1996) *Paradox, the Next Strategic Dimension: Using Conflict to Re-energize Your Business* (London: McGraw-Hill).

Mitroff, I.I., and H. Linstone (1993) *The Unbound Mind: Breaking the Chains of Traditional Business Thinking* (Oxford: Oxford University Press).

Morin, E.M. (1995) 'Organizational Effectiveness and the Meaning of Work', in T. Pauchant (ed.), *In Search of Meaning: Managing for the Health of Our Organizations, Our Communities, and the Natural World* (San Francisco: Jossey-Bass): 29-64.

Nicoll, M. (1957) *Psychological Commentaries on the Teaching of G.I. Gurdjieff and P.D. Ouspensky* (London: Vincent Stuart).

O'Donohue, J. (1998) *Anam Cara: A Book of Celtic Wisdom* (New York: Harper Perennial).

—— (2000) *Eternal Echoes: Exploring our Hunger to Belong* (London: Bantam Books).

O'Reilley, M.R. (1998) *Radical Presence: Teaching as Contemplative Practice* (Portsmouth, NH: Heinemann).

Overell, S. (2009) *Inwardness: The Rise of Meaningful Work* (Provocation Series 4.2.; London: The Work Foundation).

Paine, L. Sharp (2003) *Value Shift: Why Companies Must Merge Social and Financial Imperatives to Achieve Superior Performance* (New York: McGraw-Hill).

Palmer, P. (1990) *The Active Life: A Spirituality of Work, Creativity and Caring* (San Francisco: Jossey-Bass).

—— (2004) *A Hidden Wholeness: The Journey Toward an Undivided Life* (San Francisco: Jossey-Bass).

Parry, K.W., and A. Bryman (2006) 'Leadership in Organizations', in S.R. Clegg, C. Hardy, T.B. Lawrence and W.R. Nord (eds.), *The Sage Handbook of Organization Studies* (London: Sage, 2nd edn): 447-68.

Pauchant, T.C. (ed.) (1995). *In Search of Meaning: Managing for the Health of Our Organizations, Our Communities, and the Natural World* (San Francisco: Jossey-Bass).

Pozzi, D., and S. Williams (1998) *Success with Soul: New Insights to Achieving Success with Real Meaning* (Melbourne, VIC: Dorian Welles Proprietary).

Pruzan, P., and K. Pruzan Mikkelsen (2007) *Leading with Wisdom: Spiritual-based Leadership in Business* (Sheffield, UK: Greenleaf Publishing).

Quinn, R.E. (1988) *Beyond Rational Management: Mastering the Paradoxes and Competing Demands of High Performance* (San Francisco: Jossey-Bass).

Ready, D., and J. Conger (2008) 'Enabling Bold Visions', *MIT Sloan Management Review*, 1 January 2008.

Robinson, J.P., G. Godbey and R.D. Putnam (1999) *Time for Life: The Surprising Ways Americans Use Their Time* (University Park, PA: Pennsylvania State University Press).

Rosso, B., K. Dekas and A. Wrzesniewski (2010) 'On the Meaning of Work: A Theoretical Integration and Review', *Research in Organizational Behavior* 30: 91-127.

Scharmer, O. (2007) *Theory U: Leading from the Future as it Emerges* (San Francisco: Berrett-Koehler).

Scheuerman, W.E. (2010) 'Citizenship and Speed', in H. Rosa and W.E. Scheuerman (eds.), *High-Speed Society: Social Acceleration, Power and Modernity* (University Park, PA: Pennsylvania State University): 287-306.

Schumacher, E.F. (1978) *A Guide for the Perplexed* (London: Sphere).

Schwartz, H.S. (1995) 'Acknowledging the Dark Side of Organizational Life', in T.C. Pauchant (ed.), *In Search of Meaning: Managing for the Health of Our Organizations, Our Communities, and the Natural World* (San Francisco: Jossey-Bass): 224-43.

Senge, P. (1997) *The Fifth Discipline* (London: Century).

—— (2010) *The Necessary Revolution: Working Together to Create a Sustainable World* (New York: Broadway Books).

——, O. Scharmer, J. Jaworksi and B. Flowers (2004) *Presence: Human Purpose and the Field of the Future* (Cambridge, MA: Society for Organizational Learning).

Sennett, R. (2006) *The Culture of New Capitalism* (New Haven, CT: Yale University Press).

Sievers, B. (1994) *Work, Death and Life Itself: Essays on Management and Organization* (Berlin: Walter de Gruyter).

Sykes, K. (2007) 'The Quality of Public Dialogue', *Science* 318.5855: 1,349.

Vaill, P.B. (1996) *Learning as a Way of Being: Strategies for Survival in a World of Permanent White Water* (San Francisco: Jossey-Bass).

Wheatley, M. (2002) *Turning to One Another: Simple Conversations to Restore Hope to the Future* (San Francisco: Berrett-Koehler).

Williamson, M. (1992) *A Return to Love: Reflections on the Principles of a Course in Miracles* (New York: HarperCollins).

Willmott, H. (1993) 'Strength is Ignorance; Slavery is Freedom: Managing Culture in Modern Organizations', *Journal of Management Studies* 40.4: 515-52.

Yalom, I.D. (1980) *Existential Psychotherapy* (New York: Basic Books).

Index

Page references for figures and tables are given in *italics*.